Thoreau Country

THOREAU COUNTRY

*Photographs and Text Selections
from the Works of H. D. Thoreau
by HERBERT W. GLEASON*

Edited by MARK SILBER
Introduction by PAUL BROOKS

SIERRA CLUB BOOKS *San Francisco* 1975

Acknowledgments are due to Gail Stewart for her help with the preparation of the text and to Roland W. Robbins, owner of the Herbert W. Gleason photographic collection, for making available his resources and for his expert advice.

Selections from the writings of Henry David Thoreau conform to the text published in the 1906 edition of *The Writings of Henry David Thoreau*, published by Houghton Mifflin Company.

Library of Congress Cataloging in Publication Data

Gleason, Herbert Wendell, 1855–1937.
 Thoreau Country.

 (The Sierra Club exhibit format series)
 Includes selections from the works of H. D. Thoreau.
 1. Thoreau, Henry David, 1817–1862—Homes and
haunts. 2. New England—Description and travel—
Views. 3. Gleason, Herbert Wendell, 1855–1937.
I. Thoreau, Henry David, 1817–1862. Selections. 1975.
II. Title.
PS3053.G48 1975   818′.3′09 [B]   75-8865
ISBN 0-87156-140-9
ISBN 0-87156-144-1 pbk.

PRINTED IN THE UNITED STATES OF AMERICA.

The Sierra Club, founded in 1892 by John Muir, has devoted itself to the study and protection of the nation's scenic and ecological resources—mountains, woodlands, wild shores and rivers. All Club publications are part of the nonprofit effort the Club carries on as a public trust. There are some 50 chapters coast to coast, in Canada, Hawaii and Alaska. Participation is invited in the Club's program to enjoy and preserve wilderness everywhere. Address: 1050 Mills Tower, San Francisco, California 94104.

Contents: *Preface vii · Thoreau's Joyful Search for Truth xi · Map of*

Preface: Herbert W. Gleason and Thoreau Country

THE PUBLICATION of *Thoreau Country* is the result of several uncanny accidents—as if some power had reserved out of the myriad possibilities for the disposition of Herbert W. Gleason's long-missing work only that fate which would have satisfied Gleason's own aesthetic premises. His photography of Thoreau country was an effort to record the inspiration of a literary work concluded a half-century before him. Another half-century would pass before publication would recover Gleason's work. This unique form of literary history thus becomes, for us, a record of a part of America's past as well. In its publication is the echo of Thoreau's observation of the lilacs beside the cellar hole, which tell "their story to the retired wanderer a half-century after [the children who watered them] were no more."

In 1899, Herbert Wendell Gleason, then forty-four years old, withdrew from the ministry. At the same time he began a career as a photographer. Attracted to the writings of Thoreau and to Thoreau the man, he devoted a goodly portion of the following twenty-one years to retracing Thoreau's footsteps and photographing exactly what the writer recorded in his books and journals.

Gleason's photographic work became known early in his career, and in 1906 approximately 120 of his photographs illustrated the twenty-volume Walden edition of *The Writings of Henry David Thoreau*, edited by Bradford Torrey and Francis H. Allen. In 1917 he prepared his own photographic record of his Thoreauvian travels, called *Through the Year with Thoreau*. However, another work in progress, one larger in scope and ambition, to be called "Thoreau's World," was put aside. By 1920 Gleason had assembled at least 1,230 negatives of Thoreau country. He had achieved success as a photographer in his time. But after 1920 his interest in publishing seemed to dwindle, and in 1937 his enormous collection of glass negatives apparently disappeared, and along with them any public interest in Gleason's work.

The known biographical facts of Gleason's life are limited to the public ones. He was born in Malden, Massachusetts, on June 5, 1855; he attended Williams College and Union and Andover Seminaries. He became a Congregational minister in 1883, the year he married Lulu Rounds, a descendant of Governor Bradford of the Plymouth Colony. Sixteen years later he embraced a new life as a photographer, conservationist, and naturalist.

Drawn to the wilderness, Gleason traveled extensively and arduously—carrying the bulky camera equipment of his time. When he was preparing the introduction to *Through the Year with Thoreau* he wrote: "Lest any should assume that the fondness for New England scenery here avowed is due to lack of acquaintance with other regions more famous for their grandeur, it may be stated that during this same period the writer made two trips to Alaska, six to California and the Pacific Coast, three to the Grand Canyon of Arizona, seven to the Canadian Rockies, two to Yellowstone Park, and three to the Rocky Mountains of Colorado."

Gleason, a dedicated conservationist, was appointed an Interior Department inspector by Stephen Mather, the first director of the National Park Service. Gleason's task was to photograph and observe the existing national park areas and those lands proposed for national park status. Probably falling into that category of conservationist sometimes pejoratively called a "preservationist," Gleason with his strong historical instinct saw parks as much more than recreation areas. They were places where a human being could step directly into the flow of natural history, unspoiled and as it had been for eons. He helped to preserve many of these wilderness areas both in photographic record and through lectures and slide shows designed to promote their protection. In April 1908 in Boston, for example, he presented an illustrated lecture entitled "The Glories of the Sierras" to members and friends of the Appalachian Mountain Club. He was well acquainted with the recently founded Sierra Club, and in 1905 climbed Mt. Rainier with a Sierra Club party. Gleason's photographs appeared in *National Geographic* (his first efforts were rejected by Dr. Gilbert A. Grosvenor, then president and editor of the National Geographic Society, because they contained no man or man-made object to indicate scale). In addition to his work on Thoreau, he illustrated John Muir's *Travels in Alaska* (1915).

His very active professional life also included friendship with Luther Burbank, whom he photographed performing his horticultural experiments—a relationship which spurred Gleason's own botanical interests. He was the official photographer for the prestigious Arnold Arboretum in Boston, and continued his traveling, exploring Western North America in thirty separate trips, covering Alaska, the

Pacific Coast, the Grand Canyon, and the Rockies, from Canada to Colorado.

Little more is known about Gleason's life. There are travel schedules, publications, notations for the photographs, but as yet no glimpse into the private man. A minister who left the ministry at forty-four for reasons of health—afterwards a superb photographer, naturalist, indefatigable hiker and climber, and conservationist. He shared with Thoreau a dedication to nature that was passionate—even compassionate—and at the same time scientific. In 1930 the Gleasons' Christmas card, illustrated by a Gleason photograph, read:

"In sending thus early to all our friends, East and West, our Christmas greetings and best wishes for a Happy New Year, we beg to make one request: Will you not, in planning your Christmas decorations, avoid using Mountain Laurel, Ground Pine, American Holly, and (in California) Toyon? Ruthless and commercial gathering has in many places practically exterminated these beautiful evergreens. Other material, in large variety and equally decorative, can be secured, and some of it is surprisingly durable. For instance, a wreath of native Spruce kept its shape perfectly in our home for over three months. Yours, for the Conservation of Natural Beauty."

Gleason's wife died in 1934. He died in 1937. They left no children.

In 1945, Roland W. Robbins, a "digger of history," was trying to find the site of Thoreau's cabin by Walden Pond. As Robbins photographed the progress of the dig, he took the prints to the A. D. Handy film supply company on Bromfield Street in Boston for processing into glass slides. Robbins, later to become a president of the Thoreau Society, did establish the Walden site. A year or so later, Kenneth MacDonald, the owner of A. D. Handy, called Robbins to tell him that he had discovered a large number of old negatives that a Rev. Herbert W. Gleason had taken of Walden Pond and other subjects relating to Thoreau. Would Robbins be interested in buying them? For the sum of $100, Robbins bought the negatives, 1,230 of them, and noticed that each envelope containing a negative also contained a written reference to the passage in Thoreau being illustrated. In late 1947 Robbins heard again from the A. D. Handy Company. They were moving from the address they had occupied since the late nineteenth century and more boxes of Gleason negatives had turned up. With this unexpected addition to his Gleason collection, Robbins had approximately 6,000 photographic negatives consisting of the following subjects: Thoreau country; national park areas in the United States; Canada and Alaska; Luther Burbank and his experiments; the missions of California; Cape Cod; formal gardens in Massachusetts, Rhode Island, Connecticut, and Long Island; horticultural shows at the Arnold Arboretum; house in-

teriors; and one of Gleason's favorite subjects, individual flowers. All were carefully identified.

Robbins stored away the collection of negatives. His archaeological commitments occupied him; he recovered the remains of the Saugus Ironworks; identified the site of John Alden's house in Duxbury, Massachusetts; excavated the site of Thomas Jefferson's birthplace, Shadwell, Virginia; found the ancient docks at Strawbery Banke, Portsmouth, New Hampshire; and worked on many other early American historical sites.

In 1970, Barre Publishers in Barre, Massachusetts, expressed interest in the collection. A half-century, more in the case of many of the negatives, had passed since their creation. Barre Publishers published two books of Gleason photographs: *Thoreau's Cape Cod* and *The Western Wilderness of North America*, in 1971 and 1972 respectively. About the same time, the Sierra Club became interested in the Gleason collection, particularly the Thoreau country material. And then, to add to the sudden renascence of interest in Gleason, Princeton University Press, preparing the authoritative edition of the works of Thoreau, also became interested. The first two volumes of the recent Princeton editions, *The Illustrated Walden* and *The Illustrated Maine Woods*, contained reproductions of Gleason photographs.

Thoreau Country remained to be done. What Gleason envisaged as the final, triumphant work to be based on his 1,230 negatives, one can only surmise. Printing all in one or many volumes would not serve the photographer. But at least one other approach remained: the presentation of a distillation of Thoreau country, produced as handsomely as possible, in large format, with especial attention given to the printing of the negatives and the reproduction of the photographs, and the matching of image to text so that the camera eye of Gleason merged with Thoreau's mind's eye.

The editing and printing of the photographs for this book by photographic editor Mark Silber was not easy. The task was to select the best of the best. Silber noted: "This photographer not only presented the interpretation and location of Thoreau's description, but much more than that, he obtained a consistency of quality. This quality is rarely present in such a large body of work accomplished at the beginning of this century." Silber contact-printed each image in this book. The few underexposed negatives were printed on four grade paper. The bright areas were burned in where necessary (predominantly in those instances where Gleason indicated he wished to portray the effects of clouds, but, because of the lack of modern filters, achieved only a high contrast between the areas of sky and foreground). The halftones in this book were produced by a fine screen duotone process, in black and gray, in order to retain the precision of detail present in the plates.

Gleason's photographic work is presently being rediscovered and evaluated. The editor of this book believes that in the context of functional photographic development his work should be considered with that of Mathew Brady, Lewis Hine, and the "social documentary" photographers of the 1930s. Although little of his work interprets the face or activities of man, his photographs for the National Park Service were a motivating force behind the establishment of new areas as wildlife preserves and as national parks. This achievement in the realm of environmental preservation could be compared with the work of Jacob August Riis and Lewis Hine, who used the camera as an instrument to correct social injustice. Gleason's photography has helped to preserve wilderness which otherwise might have been doomed.

Paul Brooks's introduction about Thoreau's joyful search for truth not only sets the mood of this book but also suffices as a description of H. W. Gleason's search. The poet William Blake observed a world in a grain of sand; his reader shares the expression of that observation but not the inspiration. But here, we propose, in the juxtaposition of visual and written image, is the beginning and end, inspiration and expression, embracing. And, although the artists lived in different times, the unchanged landscape they loved connected them securely. That correspondence of verbal and visual image created a country we can never know but can recognize immediately.

JON BECKMANN
Editor-in-Chief, Sierra Club Books
San Francisco

Introduction: Thoreau's Joyful Search for Truth

IN THE LONG RUN men hit only what they aim at," wrote Henry David Thoreau in *Walden.* "Therefore . . . they had better aim at something high." He himself aimed at nothing less than a perfect correspondence of man to nature. He never achieved it, of course. But his record of the glorious attempt in the woods and fields around Concord, Massachusetts, speaks more directly to us than all the modern weighty arguments for a new view of nature as the price of survival. No wonder he is being read—notably by the young—as never before.

Born in Concord in 1817, Thoreau came naturally to his taste for the outdoors. In the words of a family friend, he "was not a superior scion on inferior stock; neither was he begotten of the northwest wind as many have supposed." His father was poor but respectable, his mother brainy and bustling, known as the most talkative woman in town. Both liked to take the children to the banks of the Assabet River, to Fair Haven Bay and Walden Pond, to Lee's Hill, where, it is said, one of them narrowly escaped being born. With the help of scholarships, they put Henry through Harvard. In his commencement "part" he suggested, in defiance of the Puritan ethic, that "the world is more to be enjoyed than used."

While still in his teens, Thoreau had read Ralph Waldo Emerson's personal declaration of independence entitled *Nature,* his first published book, written only two years after his arrival in Concord. It could not have come at a better moment. Eloquently and convincingly, it argued for freedom from literary bondage to Europe, for self-reliance—which in fact meant cultivation of one's own genius, relying on the presence of God in every man. To hold to such a lofty standard, Emerson depended throughout his life on one never-failing source of strength and inspiration: the world of nature. It was not the wild nature that early naturalist-explorers like André Michaux and William Bartram had found in the rugged Appalachians and the trackless swamps of Florida, that John James Audubon was at this moment experiencing in the American primeval forests and the windswept coasts of Labrador, that John Muir was to find amid the glaciers of Alaska. Nor as picturesque scenery could the valley of sluggish Musketaquid, the cliffs of Fair Haven Hill, the distant view of Wachusett and Monadnock be compared to the mellow grandeur of

England's Lake Country which had inspired the native poetry of William Wordsworth. Yet this quiet Concord region nurtured the genius of Emerson and Thoreau, of Hawthorne, of the Alcott family, until it came to rival Boston as the literary capital of America. In every case the fact that the writer was living close to the land, in a quiet village apart from—though within reach of—the turmoil of the city, shaped the style and substance of his work. Climbing the cliff above Fair Haven Bay with young Henry Thoreau, watching the stars to the music of the hylas in the swamp, Emerson felt no hankering for vast landscapes, the sea, or Niagara. Concord would suffice.

It would suffice for Thoreau in a deeper sense than Emerson ever knew. In all American literature there is no writer so directly, so fiercely concerned, not simply with the abstract concept of Nature, but with the living land itself. Emerson might have written happily—though differently—had he lived in a city; Thoreau never. The relationship between the two men, personal and literary, is unique. Thoreau progressed rapidly from the role of disciple to an unruly embodiment of the older man's ideas. "Thoreau gives me, in flesh and blood . . . my own ethics. His is far more real, in daily practically obeying them, than I." In fact, Thoreau obeyed his own instincts, which led him out of the study into the open, out of tame country into wild, out of the comforting, man-centered cosmos of his time into an unknown—and perhaps unknowable—universe.

It was a period of intellectual and spiritual ferment: the half-century from 1815 to 1865 that Van Wyck Brooks has called "the flowering of New England." More and more young men in Boston and elsewhere were revolting against the complacent, prosperous, materialistic society of urban America. A passion for learning went along with a new social awareness. Schools were being revolutionized, religious doctrines were being questioned, "lyceums" were drawing crowds from all classes to share the latest ideas on philosophy, literature, science. Restless students were dropping out of college to seek truth in their own fashion. Dr. William Ellery Channing, Boston's saintly preacher, shared with his friends Wordsworth and Coleridge a mystical sense of the divinity of nature; his nephew and namesake, who would become Henry Thoreau's closest companion, left Harvard to live in a log cabin on the prairie before settling down in

Concord. Thoreau's school friend and college roommate, Charles Stearns Wheeler (grandson of Dr. Charles Stearns, Lincoln's beloved pastor and romantic poet) built himself a hut on the shores of Flint's Pond in Lincoln while still an undergraduate; there Thoreau joined him for six weeks during a summer vacation and so got the idea for the later experiment at Walden.

Much of this protest has a familiar ring. The doctrine that came to be known as transcendentalism sought truth through immediate perception, transcending the learning process; one cannot help thinking of Zen. Utopian communes like Brook Farm and Fruitlands glorified rural living, vegetarianism, and contact with the soil. Long hair, bright blouses proclaimed freedom from convention; if there were fewer guitars, there were flutes. The very words echo across more than a century. "I want my place, my own place, my true place in the world," wrote Nathaniel Hawthorne, "my proper sphere, my thing. . . ."

In Concord, living with his parents and an intimate of the Emerson household, Thoreau set about enjoying the world in his own way, sometimes with Emerson or Ellery Channing, but best of all alone. Afternoons were for walking, and it was a serious business. "It required a direct dispensation from heaven to become a walker. . . . I spend four hours a day at least . . . sauntering through the woods and over the hills and fields, absolutely free from all worldly engagements." That word "sauntering" can be misleading. It is derived, Thoreau believed, from those people who roved the country in the Middle Ages, asking charity on the pretense that they were going to the Holy Land, *à la Sainte Terre*: they were *Sainte-Terrers*. For Thoreau, all land was holy. The earth, the river, the sky supplied the raw materials in his search for truth. "I go out," he told Channing, "to see what I have caught in my traps which I set for facts."

Returning from a walk in early April Thoreau begins his journal entry with the comment: "How much virtue there is in simply seeing." From the neighbors he talked with, from the audiences he lectured to, he reluctantly became convinced that very few persons really see much of nature. His daily walks through the Concord countryside, avoiding the highways and the houses, seeking out the wild thickets and the swamps, were a perennial source of excitement. Always he yearned for wildness, for "a nature which I cannot put my foot through." Relentless in his quest for knowledge, he had at the same time the mystic's need for the mysterious and unexplorable. "We need to witness our own limits transgressed, and some life pasturing freely where we never wander." In literature, he felt, tameness was synonymous with dullness. The Concord region of his day could scarcely be called a wilderness, but one could still walk for miles without passing a house or crossing a road.

Indeed the landscape was in some ways wilder than it had been a generation or two earlier. Faced with competition from the rich agricultural lands of the Midwest, drained of manpower by the rising industrial towns, the "rock farms" of New England were already on the decline. Even in Concord, whose rich soil and fertile meadowlands had attracted the early settlers, fields long under cultivation were beginning to return to forest. Thoreau's beloved "Easterbrooks Country," an area of some four square miles in the northwest part of the town, was in his day entirely unoccupied; only cellar holes and crumbling chimneys marked where farmhouses once stood. He thought that it should be preserved forever as wilderness, for all to enjoy. "There is meadow and pasture and wood-lot for the town's poor. Why not a forest and a huckleberry field for the town's rich?" (More than a century after Thoreau's death, his dream has in some measure come true through the acquisition by Harvard University of the Esterbrook Woods—as it is now known—for a biological study area. Walking through these woods today, one comes across a network of stone walls that once defined the farmers' fields, and occasionally a wide-spreading old white pine which obviously took shape in full sun and open pasture land.)

By necessity, Thoreau had to find his wildness where he could, which is to say within range of his daily walks—and within himself. "It is vain to dream of a wilderness distant from ourselves," he writes in his journal. "I shall never find in the wilds of Labrador any greater wildness than in some recess in Concord, i.e., than I import into it." Thus he was able to go 'round the world by the Old Marlborough Road, and to take an even longer journey at Walden Pond. He took pride in finding his inspiration in the commonest events. He could hear "all of music" in the humming of a telegraph wire, and discover Nova Zembla in a frozen swamp. After he had been wading one day in a shallow mud-hole, he entered in his journal a superb description of a mud turtle capturing a horn pout, concluding with the comment: "I had no idea there was so much going on in Heywood's meadow." He would not, he boasted, accept "the proudest Paris" in exchange for his native village. Concord, he said, was his garden: larger and more attractive than any artificial garden he had ever read of. As Henry Miller has written of him: "He found, by opening his eyes, that life provides everything necessary for man's peace and enjoyment."

Despite his disclaimers Thoreau would, I imagine, have gone farther afield had he been able to afford it; as it was, he made the most of what was within reach. He loved the rocky slopes of Mt. Monadnock, the bleak landscape of Cape Cod, the forests of Maine. The thought of the American West filled him with longing; romantically, he saw the backwoodsman living in paradise. Emerson complained that Henry wanted to go to Oregon, not London. One

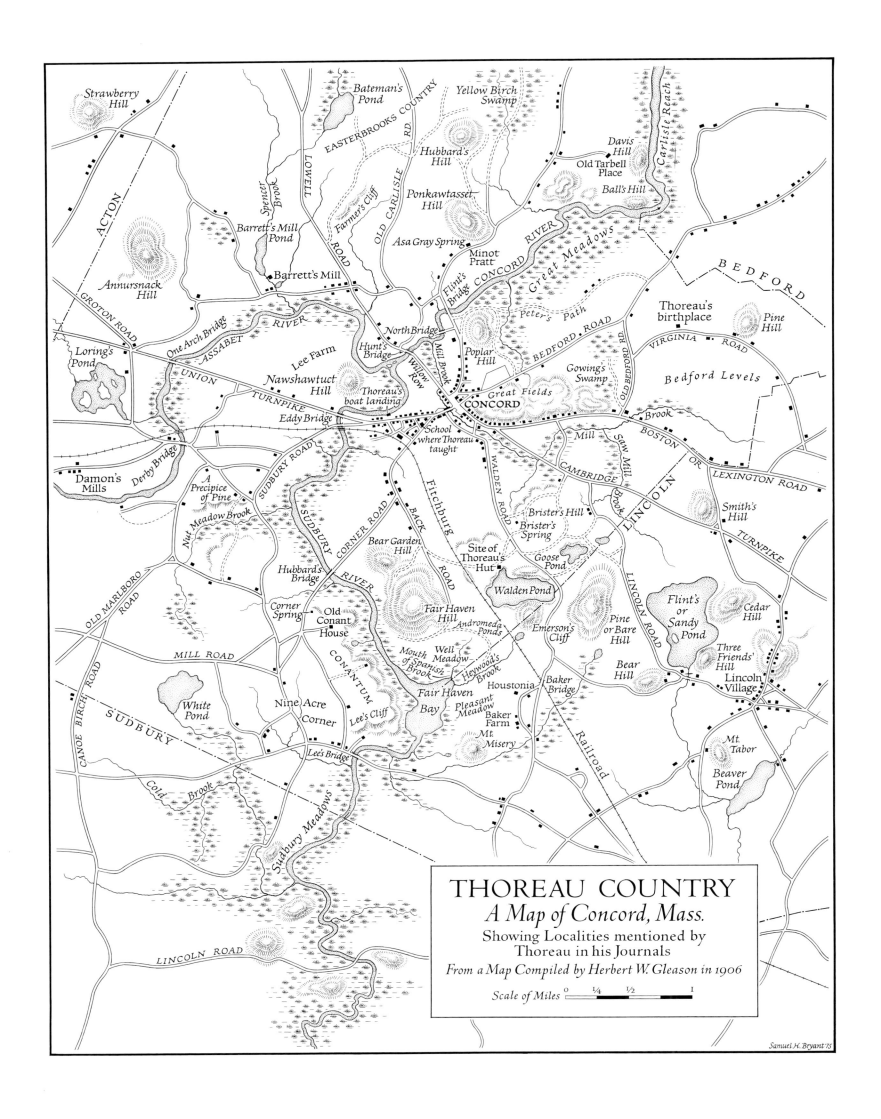

THOREAU COUNTRY
A Map of Concord, Mass.
Showing Localities mentioned by
Thoreau in his Journals
From a Map Compiled by Herbert W. Gleason in 1906

Scale of Miles   0   ¼   ½   1

Samuel H. Bryant '75

might wish that it had been Thoreau, instead of Emerson, who visited John Muir among the redwoods a decade after Thoreau's death. What a meeting that would have been! The styles of the two writers are very different: Muir ecstatic, full of superlatives; Thoreau spare, laconic. Muir was an activist, fighting for conservation, founding the Sierra Club; Thoreau was a solitary philosopher. But in their basic beliefs they were brothers. "Only by going alone in silence, without baggage," wrote Muir, "can one truly get into the heart of the wilderness." Both despised the smug belief that the world was made especially for man— a presumption, Muir remarked, not supported by the facts. Their stance was not one of misanthropy but of humility. They had too much humor to put themselves at the center of the universe.

Emerson, to whom a bird was a bird, wondered at Thoreau's knowledge of natural history. But Thoreau never thought of himself as a "scientist" in the strict sense of the word. Quite otherwise. This was an era when, as he put it, science was studied as a dead language. He hated museums with their pickled, bloated specimens; amid these corpses he felt as if he were in a tomb. A century before his time, he was concerned with the living plant, the living animal. "A man's interest in a single bluebird," he wrote to his friend Daniel Ricketson, "is worth more than a complete but dry list of the fauna and flora of a town." Yet he scorned "the mealy-mouthed enthusiasm of the mere lover of nature." As a botanist, he knew the Concord region so well that he claimed to be able to tell the day of the year from the wildflowers then in bloom; his plant collection, now pre-served at Harvard, is an invaluable source for modern scholars. While he was still in college a classmate (though finding him cold toward his fellows) described him as "Nature's own child learning to detect her wayside secrets. . . . He saw more upon the ground than anyone suspected to be there. . . ." A friend whose hobby was the study of insects complained that young Thoreau would have made a splendid entomologist if Emerson had not spoiled him.

Thoreau's view of nature—and his own relation to it—is, like his views on most subjects, replete with paradox. He feels that it is important to consider the natural world from a scientific point of view, yet equally important to ignore existing knowledge and remain open to new impressions. More than once he suggests that man cannot afford to look at nature directly; that his response is dissipated by too many observations—as indeed it is in the later volumes of his own journal. A scrupulous recorder of detail, he is never-theless repelled by too many dry facts in the scientific literature. "Oh," he exclaims, "for a little Lethe!" Ration-alizing, perhaps, his inability to identify certain songbirds (in his early years he did not even own a spyglass) he delights in hearing them sing as freshly as if it had been the first morning of creation. Always he seems torn between a passion to see, to know, to understand and—pulling him in the opposite direction—the fear that in looking too closely the vision, the poetry, will be lost. By his own admission, Thoreau was a mystic. The richest function of nature, he believed, was to symbolize human life, to become a fable or myth for man's inward experience.

For him the value of a fact was that some day it would flower into a truth—not by laborious deduction, but by "direct intercourse and sympathy." Deeply read in Oriental philosophy, he cherished his sudden moments of illumina-tion. To put Thoreau in the category of a "nature writer," as was commonly done in his time, is therefore misleading. As much as Emerson, he was a philosopher and conscious literary artist. But whereas Emerson brought the woods to his study, Thoreau brought himself to the woods. Moralizing from nature came easily to Emerson; Thoreau increasingly saw it as a weakness. "What offends me most in my com-positions is the moral element in them." Life and wildness were one; the world of nature existed for its own sake. A single hawk sailing through the upper air was worth a hundred hens. The young reader of *Nature*, the onetime disciple, had traveled far. It is hard to imagine Emerson racing a fox through the snow, or feeling a sudden impulse to eat a woodchuck raw. Nor for all his pantheism would Emerson have written about a white pine: "It is as immortal as I am, and perchance will go to as high a heaven, there to tower above me still." James Russell Lowell, then editor of the Atlantic Monthly, was shocked by such blasphemy and cut the sentence out of Thoreau's article. Thoreau never wrote for him again.

While indulging his passion for wild nature, Thoreau did not insulate himself from his fellow men. "I am naturally no hermit," he declared in *Walden*. "I think that I love society as much as most." However, his scorn of ostentation and cant drew him away from the more prosperous and pious among his neighbors toward the simple people: the farmers, the wood choppers, the hunters and the fishermen, the Irish laborers working on the railroad, and above all to the young. "This youthful, cheery figure was a familiar one in our house," wrote Edward W. Emerson, the philoso-pher's son. "When he, like the Pied Piper of Hamelin, sounded his note in the hall, the children must needs come and hug his knees, and he struggled with them, nothing loath, to the fireplace, sat down and told stories . . . of squir-rels, muskrats, hawks he had seen that day; the duel of mud-turtles in the river; the Great Homeric battle of red and black ants." Contrast this with Emerson's remark that he would as soon think of taking Henry's arm as taking the arm of an elm tree. Or with Elizabeth Hoar's telling com-ment: "I love Henry, but I don't like him." He could be prickly, notably when he felt that he was being patronized. A clergyman visiting the Thoreaus, after Henry had returned from Walden Pond, clapped him on the shoulder: "So here's the chap who camped in the woods!" Thoreau turned around: "And here's the chap that camps in a pulpit."

He idealized the concept of Woman; actual women he kept at a distance. Despite all his observations of natural behavior in the wild, and his recognition of man as a part of nature, he was squeamish about sex. Sensuality had no place in his pure image of human love. He found his ecstasies elsewhere. It has been sagely remarked that Henry Thoreau could get more out of ten minutes with a woodchuck than most men could from a night with Cleopatra.

Throughout his life Thoreau was painfully aware of his apparent coldness toward his acquaintances, and seeks to explain it to himself: "It is not that I am too cold, but that our warmth and coldness are not of the same nature; hence when I am absolutely warmest, I may be coldest to you." Again he writes with resignation in his journal: "It appears to be a law that you cannot have a deep sympathy with both man and nature. Those qualities that bring you near to the one estrange you from the other."

This, I think, is one of Thoreau's least convincing generalizations—not true even when applied to himself. Ellery Channing, who perhaps knew him best, found "no whim of coldness" in him; rather he thought of his friend as a natural stoic. Winter was his favorite season: a landscape stripped bare, trees etched in sharp silhouette against the sky. How cheerful the chime of icicles as his oar grazed the button-bushes on the river in December! Now the sound of the woodchopper's axe, the distant clarion of the cock, come clear and bell-like through the frosty air. "The wonderful purity of nature at this season is a most pleasing fact," he writes of a winter walk. "A cold and searching wind drives away all contagion." Purity. Innocence. No false notes, no soft edges, no compromise. "Better a monosyllabic life than a ragged and muttered one; let its report be short and round like a rifle, so that it may hear its own echo in the surrounding silence."

As with his life, so with his writing. The treasure that he brought back from his daily walks provided the raw material for some of the most powerful prose ever written by an American. Mere description was not enough; he sought to enjoy, in Emerson's phrase, an original relation to the universe. "Our interest depends not on the subject," he wrote near the end of his life, "but on the man, or the manner in which he treats the subject, and the importance he gives it."

In short, Thoreau was a poet, and his great poem was his journal. Here his daily observations, his speculations, his intuitions were ordered and refined, often crystallized to the point of aphorism: "How vain it is to sit down to write when you have not stood up to live!" "The best you can write will be the best you are." His love of paradox, which Emerson in the early days objected to as a literary trick, resulted at its best in the gnomic statements that sparkle through the journal: "Such naked speech is the standing aside of words to make room for thoughts."

Thoreau's method of literary composition helped him to achieve this sense of immediacy. On his daily excursions he would pause occasionally to make brief, cryptic jottings in his homemade pocket notebook, perhaps on a hillside in early March, holding his paper tight against the wind. When he returned home, he expanded these notes in his journal. Later he might review what he had written, adding "the most significant and poetic part. I do not know at first what charms me." Thoreau's double-distilled prose is at its strongest in short, taut passages: individual phrases, sentences, paragraphs. He was aware of this. In composing the final version of his journal, and the books quarried from it, he was concerned that the connecting links—if any—should be also of pure gold. Otherwise it was "better that the good be not united than that a bad man be admitted into their society." Thus in the early journals we get the sense that he was forever living in the moment, tuned to concert pitch, alert to capture the fleeting beauty of a world whose essence is impermanence. He could put all of New England spring into a single sentence: "Bluebirds' warbling curls in elms."

A poet, Thoreau believed, was one "who could impress the winds and streams into his service, to speak for him; who nailed words to their primitive senses." He used words as a cabinetmaker uses wood. He was in fact an expert carpenter. Late in life he fashioned a pine box to contain the many small notebooks that constituted his massive journal. Long after his death, when the manuscript journal was acquired by the Morgan Library, one row of notebooks appeared to fit a trifle loosely—a lapse, it would appear, from his standard of perfection. Not so. Research indicated that one notebook was missing. When it was recovered, it exactly filled the slot. His reputation was secure.

Looking into the future, Henry Thoreau wrote to a friend toward the end of his life: "What is the use of a house if you haven't got a tolerable planet to put it on?" If we do manage to maintain a tolerable planet, much credit can go to him. He did not leave us solemn sermons on conservation and ecology. He never attempted a systematic philosophy nor claimed to have discovered the ultimate truth about man's place in nature. What he has bequeathed to us through his unique genius is far more exciting: the joy of the search.

PAUL BROOKS

Ice-coated grass, shrubbery and trees, Lincoln, Massachusetts

THIS MORNING we have something between ice and frost on the trees, etc. The whole earth, as last night, but much more, is encased in ice, which on the plowed fields makes a singular icy coat a quarter of an inch or more in thickness. About 9 o'clock A.M., I go to Lee's *via* Hubbard's Wood and Holden's Swamp and the riverside, for the middle is open. The stones and cow-dung, and the walls too, are all cased in ice on the north side. The latter look like alum rocks. This, not frozen mist or frost, but frozen drizzle, collected around the slightest cores, gives prominence to the least withered herbs and grasses. Where yesterday was a plain, smooth field, appears now a teeming crop of fat, *icy* herbage. The stems of the herbs on their north sides are enlarged from ten to a hundred times. The addition is so universally on the north

side that a traveller could not lose the points of compass to-day, though it should [be] never so dark, for every blade of grass would serve to guide him, telling from which side the storm came yesterday. These straight stems of grasses stand up like white batons or sceptres, and make conspicuous foreground to the landscape, from six inches to three feet high. C. thought that these fat, icy branches on the withered grass and herbs had no nucleus, but looking closer I showed him the fine black wiry threads on which they impinged, which made him laugh with surprise. The very cow-dung is incrusted, and the clover and sorrel send up a dull-green gleam through their icy coat, like strange plants. The pebbles in the plowed land are seen as through a transparent coating of gum. Some weeds bear the ice in masses, some, like the trumpet-weed and tansy, in balls for each dried flower. What a crash of jewels as you walk! The most careless walker, who never deigned to look at these humble weeds before, cannot help observing them now. This is why the herbage is left to stand dry in the fields all winter. Upon a solid foundation of ice stand out, pointing in all directions between northwest and northeast, or within the limits of ninety degrees, little spicula or crystallized points, half an inch or more in length. . . .

Standing on the north side of a bush or tree, looking against the sky, you see only a white ghost of a tree, without a mote of earthiness, but as you go round it, the dark core comes into view. It makes all the odds imaginable whether you are travelling north or south. The drooping birches along the edges of woods are the most feathery, fairy-like ostrich plumes of the trees, and the color of their trunks increases the delusion. The weight of the ice gives to the pines the forms which northern trees, like the firs, constantly wear, bending and twisting the branches; for the twigs and plumes of the pines, being frozen, remain as the wind held them, and new portions of the trunk are exposed. Seen from the north, there is no greenness in the pines, and the character of the tree is changed. The willows along the edge of the river look like sedge in meadows. The sky is overcast, and a fine snowy hail and rain is falling, and these ghost-like trees make a scenery which reminds you of Spitzbergen. I see now the beauty of the causeway, by the bridge alders below swelling into the road, overtopped by willows and maples. The fine grasses and shrubs in the meadow rise to meet and mingle with the drooping willows, and the whole make an indistinct impression like a mist, and between this the road runs toward those white ice-clad ghostly or fairy trees in the distance,— toward spirit-land. . . .

I listen to the booming of the pond as if it were a reasonable creature. I return at last in a rain, and am coated with a glaze, like the fields.

In winter even man is to a slight extent dormant, just as some animals are but partially awake, though not commonly classed with those that hibernate. The summer circulations are to some extent stopped; the range of his afternoon walk is somewhat narrower; he is more or less confined to the highway and wood-path; the weather oftener shuts him up in his burrow; he begins to feel the access of dormancy and to assume the spherical form of the marmot; the nights are longest; he is often satisfied if he only gets out to the post-office in the course of the day. The arctic voyagers are obliged to invent and willfully engage in active amusements to keep themselves awake and alive. Most men do not now extend their walks beyond the village street. Even our experience is something like wintering in the pack.

Winter landscape from brow of Fair Haven Hill, Concord, Massachusetts

Large oak in Roundy Pasture, Lynnfield, Massachusetts

Near by, the great pasture oaks with horizontal boughs. At Pratt's, the stupendous, boughy, branching elm, like vast thunderbolts stereotyped upon the sky; heaven-defying, sending back dark vegetable bolts, as if flowing back in the channel of the lightning. The white oaks have a few leaves about the crown of the trunk in the lowest part of the tree, like a tree within a tree. The tree is thus less racked by the wind and ice.

I AM TOO LATE, perhaps, to see the sand foliage in the Deep Cut; should have been there day before yesterday; it is now too wet and soft. Yet in some places it is perfect. I see some perfect leopards' paws. These things suggest that there is motion in the earth as well as on the surface; it lives and grows. It is warmed and influenced by the sun, just as my blood by my thoughts. I seem to see some of the life that is in the spring bud and blossom more intimately, nearer its fountainhead, the fancy sketches and designs of the artist. It is more simple and primitive growth; as if for ages sand and clay might have thus flowed into the forms of foliage, before plants were produced to clothe the earth. The earth I tread on is not a dead, inert mass. It is a body, has a spirit, is organic, and fluid to the influence of its spirit, and to whatever particle of that spirit is in me. She is not dead, but sleepeth. It is more cheering than the fertility and luxuriance of vineyards, this fundamental fertility near to the principle of growth.

Sand foliage from Deep Cut, Concord, Massachusetts

This morning it is a good deal drifted. It did not freeze together, or crust, as you might have expected. You would not suppose it had been moist when it fell. About eight inches have fallen, yet there is very little on the river. It blows off, unless where water has oozed out at the sides or elsewhere, and the rough, flowing, scaly mass is frozen into a kind of batter, like mortar, or bread that has spewed out in the oven. Deep and drifted as the snow is, I found, when I returned from my walk, some dry burs of the burdock adhering to the lining of my coat. Even in the middle of winter, aye, in middle of the Great Snow, Nature does not forget these her vegetable economies.

It does look sometimes as if the world were on its last legs. How many there are whose principal employment it is nowadays to eat their meals and go to the post-office!

After spending four or five days surveying and drawing a plan incessantly, I especially feel the necessity of putting myself in communication with nature again, to recover my tone, to withdraw out of the wearying and unprofitable world of affairs. The things I have been doing have but a fleeting and accidental importance, however much men are immersed in them, and yield very little valuable fruit. I would fain have been wading through the woods and fields and conversing with the sane snow. Having waded in the very shallowest stream of time, I would now bathe my temples in eternity. I wish again to participate in the serenity of nature, to share the happiness of the river and the woods. I thus from time to time break off my connection with eternal truths and go with the shallow stream of human affairs, grinding at the mill of the Philistines; but when my task is done, with never-failing confidence I devote myself to the infinite again. It would be sweet to deal with men more, I can imagine, but where dwell they? Not in the fields which I traverse.

Pathway in the woods, near Dell Meadow, Concord, Massachusetts

Shell snowdrifts behind stone wall, Hastings, Massachusetts

To DRIFTING CUT.

The snow is now probably more than a foot deep on a level.

While I am making a path to the pump, I hear hurried *rippling* notes of birds, look up, and see quite a flock of snow buntings coming to alight amid the currant-tops in the yard. It is a sound almost as if made with their wings. What a pity our yard was made so tidy in the fall with rake and fire, and we have now no tall crop of weeds rising above this snow to invite these birds! . . .

Now, at 4:15, the blue shadows are very distinct on the snow-banks.

On the north side of the Cut, above the crossing, the jutting edges of the drift are quite handsome upon the bank. The snow is raised twelve feet above the track, and it is all scalloped with projecting eaves or copings, like turtle-shells.

They project from three to five feet, and I can stand under them. They are in three or four great layers, one lapping over another like the coarse edge of a shell. Looking along it, they appear somewhat thus:—

Often this coping has broken by its own weight, and great blocks have fallen down the bank, like smoothed blocks of white marble. The exquisite purity of the snow and the gracefulness of its curves are remarkable.

Around some houses there is not a single track. Neither man, woman, nor child, dog nor cat nor fowl, has stirred out to-day. There has been no meeting. Yet this afternoon, since the storm, it has not been very bad travelling.

Emerson's Cliff, "My Garden," Concord, Massachusetts

THE smilax (green-briar) berries still hang on like small grapes. The thorn of this vine is very perfect, like a straight dagger.

The light of the setting sun falling on the snow-banks to-day made them glow almost yellow.

The hills seen from Fair Haven Pond make a wholly new landscape; covered with snow and yellowish green or brown pines and shrub oaks, they look higher and more massive. Their white mantle relates them to the clouds in the horizon and to the sky. Perchance what is light-colored looks loftier than what is dark.

You might say of a very old and withered man or woman that they hung on like a shrub oak leaf, almost to a second spring. There was still a little life in the heel of the leaf-stalk.

Perhaps what most moves us in winter is some reminiscence of far-off summer. How we leap by the side of the open brooks! What beauty in the running brooks! What life! What society! The cold is merely superficial; it is summer still at the core, far, far within. It is in the cawing of the crow, the crowing of the cock, the warmth of the sun on our backs. I hear faintly the cawing of a crow far, far away, echoing from some unseen wood-side, as if deadened by the springlike vapor which the sun is drawing from the ground.

Heywood's Brook open in winter, Concord, Massachusetts

Snow-laden pine, Brister's Hill, Concord, Massachusetts

The value of the pitch pine in winter is that it holds the snow so finely. I see it now afar on the hillsides decking itself with it, its whited towers forming coverts where the rabbit and the gray squirrel lurk. It makes the most cheerful winter scenery beheld from the window, you know so well the nature of the coverts and the sombre light it makes.

Every man's woodlot was a miracle and surprise to him, and for those who could not go so far there were the trees in the street and the weeds in the yard. It was much like (in effect) that snow that lodges on the fine dead twigs on the lower part of a pine wood, resting there in the twilight commonly only till it has done snowing and the wind arises. But in this case it did not rest *on* the twig, but grew out from it horizontally, and it was not confined to the lowest twigs, but covered the whole forest and every surface.

Looking down the street, you might say that the scene differed from the ordinary one as frosted cake differs from plain bread. In some moods you might suspect that it was the work of enchantment. Some magician had put your village into a crucible and it had crystallized thus.

Hoar frost on trees and fence rails, Concord, Massachusetts ▶

WE turned down the brook at Heywood's meadow. It was worth the while to see how the water, even in the marsh where the brook is almost stagnant, sparkled in this atmosphere, for though warm it is remarkably clear. Water which in summer would look dark and perhaps turbid now sparkles like the lakes in November. This water is the more attractive, since all around is deep snow. The brook here is full of cat-tails (*Typha latifolia,* reed-mace). I found, on pulling open or breaking in my hand, as one would break bread, the still nearly perfect spikes of this fine reed, that the flowers were red or crimson at their base, where united to the stem. When I rubbed off thus what was at first but a thimbleful of

these dry flowerets, they suddenly took in air and flushed up like powder, expanding like feathers and foam, filling and overflowing my hand, to which they imparted a sensation of warmth quite remarkable. I was astonished to see how a small quantity was expanded and inflated on being released and given to the air, and I could not be tired with repeating the experiment. I think a single one would more than fill a half-peck measure if they lay as light as at first in the air. It is something magical to one who tries it for the first time. Like a puff of powder it flashes up. You do not know at first where they all come from. It is the conjurer's trick in nature, equal to taking feathers enough to fill a bed out of a hat. When you

Heywood's Brook open in winter, Concord, Massachusetts

Ice-coated pine needles, Lincoln, Massachusetts

had done, but still will scrape the almost bare stem, still they overflow your hand as before. See it again, and try the combustibility of the pollen. As the flowerets are opening and liberating themselves, showing their red extremities, it has the effect of a changeable color.

Ah, then, the brook beyond, its rippling waters and its sunny sands! They made me forget that it was winter. Where springs oozed out of the soft bank over the dead leaves and the green sphagnum, they had melted the snow, or the snow had melted as it fell perchance, and the rabbits had sprinkled the mud about on the snow. The sun reflected from the sandy, gravelly bottom sometimes a bright sunny streak no bigger than your finger, reflected from a ripple as from a prism, and the sunlight, reflected from a hundred points of the surface of the rippling brook, enabled me to realize summer.

Every leaf and twig was this morning covered with a sparkling ice armor; even the grasses in exposed fields were hung with innumerable diamond pendants, which jingled merrily when brushed by the foot of the traveller. It was literally the wreck of jewels and the crash of gems. It was as though some superincumbent stratum of the earth had been removed in the night, exposing to light a bed of untarnished crystals. The scene changed at every step, or as the head was inclined to the right or the left. There were the opal and sapphire and emerald and jasper and beryl and topaz and ruby.

Such is beauty ever,—neither here nor there, now nor then,—neither in Rome nor in Athens, but wherever there is a soul to admire. If I seek her elsewhere because I do not find her at home, my search will prove a fruitless one.

THE COLDEST NIGHT for a long, long time was last. Sheets froze stiff about the faces. Cat mewed to have the door opened, but was at first disinclined to go out. When she came in at nine she smelt of meadow-hay. We all took her up and smelled of her, it was so fragrant. Had cuddled in some barn. People dreaded to go to bed. The ground cracked in the night as if a powder-mill had blown up, and the timbers of the house also. My pail of water was frozen in the morning so that I could not break it. Must leave many buttons unbuttoned, owing to numb fingers. Iron was like fire in the hands. Thermometer at about 7:30 A.M. gone into the bulb, −19° at least. The cold has stopped the clock. Every bearded man in the street is a graybeard. Bread, meat, milk, cheese, etc., etc., all frozen. See the inside of your cellar door all covered and sparkling with frost like Golconda. Pity the poor who have not a large wood-pile. The latches are white with frost, and every nail-head in entries, etc., has a white cap. The chopper hesitates to go to the woods. Yet I see S. W—— stumping past, three quarters of a mile, for his morning's dram. Neighbor Smith's thermometer stood at −26° early this morning. But this day is at length more moderate than yesterday. . . .

Though the cold has been moderate to-day compared with yesterday, it has got more into the houses and barns, and the farmers complain more of it while attending to their cattle. This, *i.e.* yesterday, the 6th, will be remembered as the cold Tuesday. The old folks still refer to the Cold Friday, when they sat before great fires of wood four feet long, with a fence of blankets behind them, and water froze on the mantelpiece. But they say this is as cold as that was.

Frost work on window

Frost crystals on ice near Gilson's Camp, Jaffrey, New Hampshire

On the ice at Walden are very beautiful great leaf crystals in great profusion. The ice is frequently thickly covered with them for many rods. They seem to be connected with the rosettes,—a running together of them. They look like a loose web of small white feathers springing from a tuft of down, for their shafts are lost in a tuft of fine snow like the down about the shaft of a feather, as if a feather bed had been shaken over the ice. They are, on a close examination, surprisingly perfect leaves like ferns, only very broad for their length and commonly more on one side the midrib than the other. They are from an inch to an inch and a half long and three quarters wide, and slanted, where I look, from the southwest. They have, first, a very distinct midrib, though so thin that they cannot be taken up; then, distinct ribs branching from this, commonly opposite, and minute ribs springing again from these last, as in many ferns, the last running to each crenation in the border. How much further they are subdivided, the naked eye cannot discern. They are so thin and fragile that they melt under your breath while looking closely at them. A fisherman says they were much finer in the morning. In other places the ice is strewn with a different kind of frostwork in little patches, as if oats had been spilled, like fibres of asbestos rolled, a half or three quarters of an inch long and an eighth or more wide. Here and there patches of them a foot or two over. Like some boreal grain spilled.

I TREAD in the tracks of the fox which has gone before me by some hours, or which perhaps I have started, with such a tiptoe of expectation as if I were on the trail of the Spirit itself which resides in these woods, and expected soon to catch it in its lair.

The snow falls on no two trees alike, but the forms it assumes are as various as those of the twigs and leaves which receive it. They are, as it were, predetermined by the genius of the tree. So one divine spirit descends alike on all, but bears a peculiar fruit in each. The divinity subsides on all men, as the snowflakes settle on the fields and ledges and takes the form of the various clefts and surfaces on which it lodges.

Here is the distinct trail of a fox stretching [a] quarter of a mile across the pond. Now I am curious to know what has determined its graceful curvatures, its greater or less spaces and distinctness, and how surely they were coincident with the fluctuations of some mind, why they now lead me two steps to the right, and then three to the left. If these things are not to be called up and accounted for in the Lamb's Book of Life, I shall set them down for careless accountants. Here was one expression of the divine mind this morning. The pond was his journal, and last night's snow made a *tabula rasa* for him. I know which way a mind wended this morning, what horizon it faced, by the setting of these tracks; whether it moved slowly or rapidly, by the greater or less intervals and distinctness, for the swiftest step leaves yet a lasting trace.

Fox track in Heywood's Meadow, Concord, Massachusetts

It is a moist and starry snow, lodging on trees,—leaf, bough, and trunk. The pines are well laden with it. How handsome, though wintry, the side of a high pine wood, well grayed with the snow that has lodged on it, and the smaller pitch pines converted into marble or alabaster with their lowered plumes like rams' heads!

The character of the wood-paths is wholly changed by the new-fallen snow. Not only all tracks are concealed, but, the pines drooping over it and half concealing or filling it, it is merely a long chink or winding open space between the trees.

Heavy snow-laden tree, Concord, Massachusetts

Alder bush, Fair Haven Bay island in distance, Concord, Massachusetts

Snow-fleas lie in black patches like some of those dark rough lichens on rocks, or like ink-spots three or four inches in diameter, about the grass-stems or willows, on the ice which froze last night. When I breathe on them I find them all alive and ready to skip. Also the water, when I break the ice, arouses them. I saw yesterday, in a muddy spring in Tarbell's meadow, many cockle[*sic*]-shells on the bottom, with their feet out, and marks as if they had been moving.

When I read of the catkins of the alder and the willow, etc., scattering their yellow pollen, they impress me as a vegetation which belongs to the earliest and most innocent dawn of nature; as if they must have preceded other trees in the order of creation, as they precede them annually in their blossoming and leafing. In the winter we so value the semblance of fruit that even the dry black female catkins of the alder are an interesting sight, not to mention, on shoots rising a foot or two above these, the red or mulberry male catkins, in little parcels, dangling at a less than right angle with the stems, and the short female ones at their bases. For how many æons did the willow shed its yellow pollen annually before man was created!

Apparently I read Cato and Varro from the same motives that Virgil did, and as I read the almanac, *New England Farmer*, or *Cultivator*, or Howitt's "Seasons."

I̲ᴛ ɪs ᴀ ᴅᴀʏ for those rake and horn icicles; the water, dashing against the southeast shores where they chance to be open, *i.e.* free of ice, and blown a rod inland, freezes to the bushes, forming rakes and oftener horns. If twigs project above the ice-belt thus: the water freezes over them thus:—

The very grass stubble is completely encased for a rod in width along the shore, and the trunks of trees for two or three feet up. Any sprig lying on the edge of the ice is completely crusted. Sometimes the low button-bush twigs with their few remaining small dark balls, and also the drooping corymbs of the late rose hips, are completely encased in an icicle, and you see their bright scarlet reflected through the ice in an exaggerated manner. If a hair is held up above the ice where this spray is blowing, it is sufficient to start a thick icicle rake or horn, for the ice forming around it becomes at once its own support, and gets to be two or three inches thick. Where the open water comes within half a dozen feet of the shore, the spray has blown over the intervening ice and covered the grass and stubble, looking like a glaze,—countless loby fingers and horns over some fine stubble core,—and when the grass or stem is

horizontal you have a rake. Just as those great organ-pipe icicles that drip from rocks have an annular structure growing downward, so these on the horizontal stubble and weeds, when directed to the point toward which the wind was blowing; *i.e.*, they grow thus southeast.

Then there is the thickened edge of the ice, like a cliff, on the southeast sides of openings against which the wind has dashed the waves, especially on the southeast side of broad meadows.

No finer walking in any respect than on our broad meadow highway in the winter, when covered with bare ice. If the ice is wet, you slip in rubbers; but when it is dry and cold, rubbers give you a firm hold, and you walk with a firm and elastic step. I do not know of any more exhilarating walking than up or down a broad field of smooth ice like this in a cold, glittering winter day when your rubbers give you a firm hold on the ice.

I see that the open places froze last night only on the windward side, where they were less agitated, the waves not yet running so high there.

A little snow, however, even the mere shavings or dust of ice made by skaters, hinders walking in rubbers very much, for though the rubber may give a good hold on clear ice, when you step on a little of the ice dust or snow you slide on that.

Those little gyrinus-shaped bugs of the 8th, that had come out through a crevice in the ice about a boat frozen in, and were swimming about in the shallow water above the ice, I see are all gone now that that water is frozen,—have not been frozen in; so they must have returned back under the ice when it became cold, and this shows that they were not forced up accidentally in the first place, but attracted by the light and warmth, probably as those minnows were some time ago. That is, in a thaw in the winter some water-insects—beetles, etc.—will come up through holes in the ice and swim about in the sun.

Frozen spray on bushes at mouth of Spanish Brook, Concord, Massachusetts

To HUBBARD'S BATH.

The frost out of the ground and the ways settled in many places. I see much more of that gossamer(?) of the morning,—still regarding the large mildew as different. It abounds in all low grounds where there is a firm pasture sod, where a snow-bank has just melted or on the edge of one that is fast disappearing. I observe some remarkable ones on Hubbard's land just below the mountain sumachs. They are thin webs over the grass just laid bare close to the snow commonly and over the icy edge of the snow. They are not under the snow. I thought at first it had been formed on the surface of the snow and when it melted rested lightly on the stubble beneath, but I could detect none extending more than three or four inches over the icy edge of the snow, though every stubble half exposed amid the snow even was the source or *point d'appui* of some. Sometimes, to my surprise, it was an extremely thin, but close-woven(?), perhaps air-tight veil, of the same color but still thinner than the thinnest tissue paper or membrane, in patches one to three feet in diameter, resting lightly on the stubble, which supports it in the form of little tents. This is now dry and very brittle, yet I can get up pieces an inch across. It suggests even a scum on the edge of the melting snow, which has at last dried and hardened into a web. Here is one which, as commonly, springs from three or four inches within the melted snow, partly resting close and flat upon it, and extends thence several feet from its edge over the stubble. None of these have the thickness of mildew, and for cobwebs I see but two or three spiders about and cannot believe that they can have done all this in one night, nor do they make a close web. It lies lightly upon the stubble and the edge of the snow, as if it had settled in the night from the atmosphere. Can it be a scum formed on the melting snow, caught at last on the stubble like the pap of paper taken up in a sieve? Further off on every side I see the same now fretted away, like a coarse and worn-out sieve, where it was perfect perhaps yesterday.

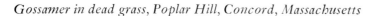

Gossamer in dead grass, Poplar Hill, Concord, Massachusetts

SPRING

Great Meadows flooded and lingering snow, Concord, Massachusetts

THE GROUND is now generally bare of snow, though it lies along walls and on the north sides of valleys in the woods pretty deep.

I LOOK DOWN over Tarbell's Bay, just north of Ball's Hill.
Not only meadows but potato and rye fields are buried deep,
and you see there, sheltered by the hills on the northwest, a
placid blue bay having the russet hills for shores. This kind
of bay, or lake, made by the freshet—these deep and narrow
"fiords"—can only be seen along such a stream as this, liable
to an annual freshet. The water rests as gently as a dewdrop
on a leaf, laving its tender temporary shores. It has no strand,
leaves no permanent water-mark, but though you look at it a
quarter of a mile off, you know that the rising flood is gently
overflowing a myriad withered green blades there in succession. There is the magic of lakes that come and go. The
lake or bay is not an institution, but a phenomenon. You
plainly see that it is so much water poured into the hollows
of the earth.

Tarbell's Bay, Concord, Massachusetts

Our woods are now so reduced that the chopping of this winter has been a cutting to the quick. At least we walkers feel it as such. There is hardly a wood-lot of any consequence left but the chopper's axe has been heard in it this season. They have even infringed fatally on White Pond, on the south of Fair Haven Pond, shaved off the topknot of the Cliffs, the Colburn farm, Beck Stow's, etc., etc.

Slaughtered pines across from Walden, Concord, Massachusetts

Pine stick etched by worms

Save with my boat the dead top of (apparently) a pine, divested of its bark and bleached. Before the bark fell off it was curiously etched by worms in variously curved lines and half-circles, often with regular short recurring branches, thus:

To WHITE POND.

Coldest day for a month or more,—severe as almost any in the winter. Saw this afternoon either a snipe or a woodcock; it appeared rather small for the last. Pond opening on the northeast. A flock of hyemalis drifting from a wood over a field incessantly for four or five minutes,—thousands of them, notwithstanding the cold. The fox-colored sparrow sings sweetly also. Saw a small slate-colored hawk, with wings transversely mottled beneath,—probably the sharp-shinned hawk.

Got first proof of "Walden."

Ice breaking up, northwest cove of Walden, Concord, Massachusetts

Skunk cabbage leafing out at Clamshell Bank, Concord, Massachusetts

I FIND many sound cabbages shedding their pollen under Clamshell Hill. They are even more forward *generally* here than at Well Meadow. Probably two or three only, now dead among the alders at the last place, were earlier. This is simply the earliest flower such a season as this, *i.e.* when the ground continues covered with snow till very late in the spring. For this plant occupies ground which is the earliest to be laid bare, those great dimples in the snow about a springy place in the meadow, five or ten feet over, where the sun and light have access to the earth a month before it is generally bare. In such localities, then, they will enjoy the advantage over most other plants, for they will not have to contend with abundance of snow, but only with the cold air, which may be no severer than usual. Cowslips and a few other plants sometimes enjoy the same advantage. Sometimes, *apparently*, the original, now outer, spathe has been frost-bitten and is decayed, and a fresh one is pushing up. I see some of these in full bloom, though the opening to their tents is not more than half an inch wide. They are lapped like tent doors, effectually protected. Methinks most of these hoods open to the south. It is remarkable how completely the spadix is protected from the weather, first by the ample hood, whose walls are distant from it, next by the narrow tent-like doorway, admitting air and light and sun, generally I think on the south side, and also by its pointed top, curved downward protectingly over it. It looks like a monk in his crypt with powdered head. The sides of the doorway are lapped or folded, and one is considerably in advance of the other. It is contrived best to catch the vernal warmth and exclude the winter's cold. Notwithstanding all the snow the skunk-cabbage is earlier than last year, when it was also the earliest flower and blossomed on the 5th of April. It is, perhaps, owing to the long-continued warm weather from March 13th to 28th.

THE EPIGÆA looks as if it would open in two or three days at least,—showing much color and this form: The flower-buds are protected by the withered leaves, oak leaves, which partly cover them, so that you must look pretty sharp to detect the first flower. These plants blossom by main strength, as it were, or the virtue that is in them,—not growing by water, as most early flowers,—in dry copses.

Arbutus, Plymouth, Massachusetts

I HEAR no hylas nor croakers in the morning. Is it too cool for them? The gray branches of the oaks, which have lost still more of their leaves, seen against the pines when the sun is rising and falling on them, how rich and interesting!

From Cliffs see on the still water under the hill, at the outlet of the pond, two ducks sailing, partly white. Hear the faint, swelling, far-off beat of a partridge.

Saw probably female red-wings (?), grayish or dark ashy-brown, on an oak in the woods, with a male (?) whose red shoulder did not appear.

How many walks along the brooks I take in the spring! What shall I call them? Lesser riparial excursions? Prairial? rivular?

When I came out there was not a speck of mist in the sky, but the morning without a cloud is not the fairest. Now, 8.30 A.M., it rains. Such is April.

Oak and brook at West Conantum Pool, Concord, Massachusetts

D. Ricketson's "shanty," New Bedford, Massachusetts

D. R.'s shanty is about half a dozen rods southwest of his house (which may be forty rods from the road), nearly between his house and barn; is twelve by fourteen feet, with seven-feet posts, with common pent-roof. In building it, he directed the carpenter to use Western boards and timber, though some Eastern studs (spruce?) were inserted. He had already occupied a smaller shanty at "Woodlee" about a mile south. The roof is shingled and the sides made of matched boards and painted a light clay-color with chocolate(?)-colored blinds. Within, it is not plastered and is open to the roof, showing the timbers and rafters and rough boards and cross-timbers overhead as if ready for plastering. The door is at the east end with a small window on each side of it; a similar window on each side the building, and one at the west end, the latter looking down the garden walk. In front of the last window is a small box stove with a funnel rising to a level with the plate, and there inserted in a small brick chimney which rests on planks. On the south side the room, against the stove, is a rude settle with a coarse cushion and pillow; on the opposite side, a large low desk, with some book-shelves above it; on the same side, by the window, a small table covered with books; and in the northeast corner, behind the door, an old-fashioned secretary, its pigeonholes stuffed with papers. On the opposite side as you enter, is place for fuel, which the boy leaves each morning, a place to hang greatcoats. There were two small pieces of carpet on the floor, and Ricketson or one of his guests swept out the shanty each morning. There was a small kitchen clock hanging in the southwest corner and a map of Bristol County behind the settle.

The west and northwest side is well-nigh covered with slips of paper, on which are written some sentence or paragraph from R.'s favorite books. I noticed, among the most characteristic, Dibdin's "Tom Tackle," a translation of Anacreon's "Cicada," lines celebrating tobacco, Milton's "How charming is divine philosophy," etc., "Inveni requiem: Spes et Fortuna valete. Nil mihi vobiscum est: ludite nunc alios" (is it Petrarch?) (this is also over the door), "Mors aequo pulsat," etc., some lines of his own in memory of A. J. Downing, "Not to be in a hurry," over the desk, and many other quotations celebrating retirement, country life, simplicity, humanity, sincerity, etc., etc., from Cowper and other English poets, and similar extracts from newspapers. There were also two or three advertisements,—one of a cattle-show exhibition, another warning not to kill birds contrary to law (he being one of the subscribers ready to enforce the act), advertisement of a steamboat on Lake Winnepiseogee, etc., cards of his business friends. The size of different brains from *Hall's Journal of Health*, and "Take the world easy." A sheet of blotted blotting-paper tacked up, and of Chinese character from a tea-chest. Also a few small pictures and pencil sketches, the latter commonly caricatures of his visitors or friends, as "The Trojan" (Channing) and "Van Best." I take the more notice of these particulars because his peculiarities are so commonly unaffected. He has long been accustomed to put these scraps on his walls and has a basketful somewhere, saved from the old shanty. Though there were some quotations which had no right there, I found all his peculiarities faithfully expressed,—his fear of death, love of retirement, simplicity, etc.

The more characteristic books were Bordley's "Husbandry," Drake's "Indians," Barber's "Historical Collections," Zimmermann on Solitude. Bigelow's "Plants of Boston, etc.," Farmer's "Register of the First Settlers of New England," Marshall's "Gardening," Nicol's "Gardener," John Woolman, "The Modern Horse Doctor," Downing's "Fruits, etc.," "The Farmer's Library," "Walden," Dymond's Essays, Job Scott's Journal, Morton's Memorial, Bailey's Dictionary, Downing's "Landscape Gardening, etc.," "The Task," Nuttall's Ornithology, Morse's Gazetteer, "The Domestic Practice of Hydropathy," "John Buncle," Dwight's Travels, Virgil, Young's "Night Thoughts," "History of Plymouth," and other "*Shanty Books*."

Hosmer's house and cottage under its elms and on the summit of green smooth slopes looks like a terrestrial paradise, the abode of peace and domestic happiness. Far over the woods westward, a shining vane, glimmering in the sun.

Hosmer Homestead, Concord, Massachusetts

THEY TOLD ME at New Bedford that one of their whalers came in the other day with a black man aboard whom they had picked up swimming in the broad Atlantic, without anything to support him, but nobody could understand his language or tell where he came from. He was in good condition and well-behaved. My respect for my race rose several degrees when I heard this, and I thought they had found the true merman at last. "What became of him?" I inquired. "I believe they sent him to the State Almshouse," was the reply. Could anything have been more ridiculous? That he should be beholden to Massachusetts for his support who floated free where Massachusetts with her State Almshouse could not have supported herself for a moment. They should have dined him, then accompanied him to the nearest cape and bidden him good-by. The State would do well to appoint an intelligent standing committee on such curious [*sic*], in behalf of philologists, naturalists, and so forth, to see that the proper disposition is made of such visitors.

Old whaling vessels, New Bedford, Massachusetts

Young hellebore plants at Corner Spring, Concord, Massachusetts

THE neatly and closely folded, plaited, leaves of the hellebore are rather handsome objects now. As you pull them apart, they emit a slight marshy scent, somewhat like the skunk-cabbage. They are tender and dewy within, folded fan-like.

MANY *Anemone nemorosa* in full bloom at the further end of Yellow Thistle Meadow, in that warm nook by the brook, some probably a day or two there. I think that they are thus early on account of Miles's dam having broken away and washed off all the snow for some distance there, in the latter part of the winter, long before it melted elsewhere. It is a warm corner under the south side of a wooded hill, where they are not often, if ever before, flooded.

As I was measuring along the Marlborough road, a fine little blue-slate butterfly fluttered over the chain. Even its feeble strength was required to fetch the year about. How daring, even rash, Nature appears, who sends out butterflies so early! Sardanapalus-like, she loves extremes and contrasts.

Wood anemones, Concord, Massachusetts

Lilacs at side of old Conantum house, Concord, Massachusetts

Now only a dent in the earth marks the site of most of these human dwellings; sometimes the well-dent where a spring oozed, now dry and tearless grass, or covered deep,— not to be discovered till late days by accident,—with a flat stone under the sod. These dents, like deserted fox-burrows, old holes, where once was the stir and bustle of human life overhead, and man's destiny, "fate, free-will, foreknowledge absolute," were all by turns discussed.

Still grows the vivacious lilac for a generation after the last vestige else is gone, unfolding still its early sweet-scented blossoms in the spring, to be plucked only by the musing traveller; planted, tended, weeded [?], watered by children's hands in front-yard plot,—now by wall-side in retired pasture, or giving place to a new rising forest. The last of that stirp, sole survivor of that family. Little did the dark children think that that weak slip with its two eyes which they watered would root itself so, and outlive them, and house in the rear that shaded it, and grown man's garden and field, and tell their story to the retired wanderer a half-century after they were no more,—blossoming as fair, smelling as sweet, as in that first spring. Its still cheerful, tender, civil lilac colors.

Sit on the steep north bank of White Pond. The *Amelanchier Botryapium* in flower now spots the brown sprout-land hillside on the southeast side, across the pond, very interestingly. Though it makes but a faint impression of color, I see its pink distinctly a quarter of a mile off. It is seen now in sprout-lands half a dozen years old, where the oak leaves have just about all fallen except a few white oaks. (It is in prime about the 8th [May].) Others are seen directly under the bank on which we sit, on this side, very white against the blue water.

Many at this distance would not notice those shadbush flowers on the hillside, or [would] mistake them for whitish rocks. They are the more interesting for coming thus between the fall of the oak leaves and the expanding of other shrubs and trees. Some of the larger, near at hand, are very light and elegant masses of white bloom. The white-fingered flower of the sprout-lands. In sprout-lands, having probably the start or preëminence over the other sprouts, from not being commonly, or [at] all, cut down with the other trees and shrubs, they are as high or higher than any of them for five or six years, and they are so early that they feel almost the full influence of the sun, even amid full-grown deciduous trees which have not leafed, while they are considerably sheltered from the wind by them.

Shad-bush in bloom, near Baker's Bridge, Concord, Massachusetts

A PARTRIDGE-NEST, with eleven fresh eggs, at foot of a chestnut, one upon another. It is quite a deep cavity amid the leaves, with some feathers of the bird in it.

Partridge nest near Brister's Spring, Concord, Massachusetts

THERE ARE some dense beds of houstonia in the yard of the old Conantum house. Some parts of them show of a distinctly bluer shade two rods off. They are most interesting now, before many other flowers are out, the grass high, and they have lost their freshness. I sit down by one dense bed of them to examine it. It is about three feet long and two or more wide. The flowers not only crowd one another, but are in several tiers, one above another, and completely hide the ground,—a mass of white. Counting those in a small place, I find that there are about three thousand flowers in a square foot. They are all turned a little toward the sun, and emit a refreshing odor. Here is a lumbering humblebee, probing these tiny flowers. It is a rather ludicrous sight. Of course they will not support him, except a little where they are densest; so he bends them down rapidly (hauling them in with his arms, as it were), one after another, thrusting his beak into the tube of each. It takes him but a moment to dispatch one. It is a singular sight, a humblebee clambering over a bed of these delicate flowers. There are various other bees about them.

Large cluster of houstonia, near Baker's Bridge, Concord, Massachusetts

ARUM TRIPHYLLUM out. Almost every one has a little fly or two concealed within. One of the handsomest-formed plants when in flower. Sorrel out in rain, apparently a day or two,—say 9th. A blue heron flies away from the shore of the pond.

Jack-in-the-pulpit, Concord, Massachusetts

Houses along the road up Bellow's Pipe, Williamstown, Massachusetts

IT IS PLEASANT when the road winds along the side of a hill with a thin fringe of wood through which to look into the low land. It furnishes both shade and frame for your pictures,—as this Corner road.

Apple trees in bloom on Conantum Road, Concord, Massachusetts

Yesterday, when I walked to Goodman's Hill, it seemed to me that the atmosphere was never so full of fragrance and spicy odors. There is a great variety in the fragrance of the apple blossoms as well as their tints. Some are quite spicy. The air seemed filled with the odor of ripe strawberries, though it is quite too early for them. The earth was not only fragrant but sweet and spicy to the smell, reminding us of Arabian gales and what mariners tell of the spice islands. The first of June, when the lady's-slipper and the wild pink have come out in sunny places on the hillsides, then the summer is begun according to the clock of the seasons.

Moon reflection in river over Fair Haven Hill from bridge, Concord, Massachusetts

LAY ON A ROCK near a meadow, which had absorbed and retained much heat, so that I could warm my back on it, it being a cold night. I found that the side of the sand-hill was cold on the surface, but warm two or three inches beneath.

If there is a more splendid moonlight than usual, only the belated traveller observes it. When I am outside, on the outskirts of the town, enjoying the still majesty of the moon, I am wont to think that all men are aware of this miracle, that they too are silently worshipping this manifestation of divinity elsewhere. But when I go into the house I am undeceived; they are absorbed in checkers or chess or novel, though they may have been advertised of the brightness through the shutters.

In the moonlight night what intervals are created! The rising moon is related to the near pine tree which rises above the forest, and we get a juster notion of distance. The moon is only somewhat further off and on one side. There may be only three objects,—myself, a pine tree, and the moon, nearly equidistant.

Talk of demonstrating the rotation of the earth on its axis,—see the moon rise, or the sun!

The moonlight reveals the beauty of trees. By day it is so light and in this climate so *cold* commonly, that we do not perceive their shade. We do not know when we are beneath them.

Young birch leafing out in spring, Concord, Massachusetts

Most trees are beautiful when leafing out, but especially the birch. After a storm at this season, the sun comes out and lights up the tender expanding leaves, and all nature is full of light and fragrance, and the birds sing without ceasing, and the earth is a fairyland. The birch leaves are so small that you see the landscape through the tree, and they are like silvery and green spangles in the sun, fluttering about the tree.

Now the sun has come out after the May storm, how bright, how full of freshness and tender promise and fragrance is the new world! The woods putting forth new leaves; it is a memorable season. So hopeful! These young leaves have the beauty of flowers. The shrub oaks are just beginning to blossom. The forward leaves and shoots of the meadow-sweet, beneath the persistent dead flowers, make a very rich and conspicuous green now along the fences and walls. The conspicuous white flowers of the two kinds of shad-blossom spot the hillsides at a distance. This is the only bush or tree whose flowers are sufficiently common and large at this time (to-day), except the *Salix alba* and the peach (the choke-cherry is rare), to make a show now, as the apples will soon. I see dark pines in the distance in the sunshine, contrasting with the light fresh green of the deciduous trees.

There is life in these fresh and varied colors, life in the motion of the wind and the waves; all make it a flowing, washing day.

May foliage, Conantum pasture, Concord, Massachusetts

Thoreau's rock shelter at Lee's Cliff, Concord, Massachusetts

I SEE through the tree-tops the thin vanguard of the storm sealing the celestial ramparts, like eager light infantry, or cavalry with spears advanced. But from the west a great, still, ash-colored cloud comes on. The drops fall thicker, and I seek a shelter under the Cliffs. I stand under a large projecting portion of the Cliff, where there is ample space above and around, and I can move about as perfectly protected as under a shed. To be sure, fragments of rock look as if they would fall, but I see no marks of recent ruin about me.

Soon I hear the low all-pervading hum of an approaching hummingbird circling above the rock, which afterward I mistake several times for the gruff voices of men approaching, unlike as these sounds are in some respects, and I perceive the resemblance even when I know better. Now I am sure it is a hummingbird, and now that it is two farmers approaching. But presently the hum becomes more sharp and thrilling, and the little fellow suddenly perches on an ash twig within a rod of me, and plumes himself while the rain

Lady's slippers, Concord, Massachusetts

is fairly beginning. He is quite out of proportion to the size of his perch. It does not acknowledge his weight.

I sit at my ease and look out from under my lichen-clad rocky roof, half-way up the Cliff, under freshly leafing ash and hickory trees on to the pond, while the rain is falling faster and faster, and I am rather glad of the rain, which affords me this experience. The rain has compelled me to find the cosiest and most homelike part of all the Cliff.

Everywhere now in dry pitch pine woods stand the red lady's-slippers over the red pine leaves on the forest floor, rejoicing in June, with their two broad curving green leaves,—some even in swamps. Uphold their rich, striped red, drooping sack. This while rye begins to wave richly in the fields.

SUMMER

Fog from Nawshawtuct, Concord, Massachusetts

To NAWSHAWTUCT.

I go to the river in a fog through which I cannot see more than a dozen rods,—three or four times as deep as the houses. As I row down the stream, the dark, dim outlines of the trees on the banks appear, coming to meet me out of the mist on the one hand, while they retreat and are soon concealed in it on the other. My strokes soon bury them behind me. The birds are wide awake, as if knowing that this fog presages a fair day. I ascend Nawshawtuct from the north side. I am aware that I yield to the same influence which inspires the birds and the cockerels, whose hoarse courage I hear now vaunted. So men should crow in the morning. I would crow like chanticleer in the morning, with all the lustiness that the new day imparts, without thinking of the evening, when I and all of us shall go to roost,—with all the humility of the cock, that takes his perch upon the highest rail and wakes the country with his clarion. Shall not men be inspired as much as cockerels? My feet are soon wet with fog. It is, indeed, a vast dew. And are not the clouds another kind of dew? Cool nights produce them.

Now I have reached the hilltop above the fog at a quarter to five, about sunrise, and all around me is a sea of fog, level and white, reaching nearly to the top of this hill, only the tops of a few high hills appearing as distant islands in the main. Wachusett is a more distant and larger island, an Atlantis in the west; there is hardly one to touch at between me and it. It is just like the clouds beneath you as seen from a mountain. It is a perfect level in some directions, cutting the hills near their summits with a geometrical line, but puffed up here and there, and more and more toward the east, by the influence of the sun. An early freight-train of cars is heard, not seen, rushing through the town beneath it. It resembles nothing so much as the ocean. You can get here the impression which the ocean makes, without ever going to the shore. Men—poor simpletons as they are—will go to a panorama by families, to see a Pilgrim's Progress, perchance, who never yet made progress so far as to the top of such a hill as this at the dawn of a foggy morning. All the fog they know is in their brains.

Old elm on Lee Farm, Concord, Massachusetts

I WAS INTERESTED in the old elm near the southeast corner of the house, which I found had been a mere shell a few years since, now filled up with brick. Flood, who has lived there, told me that Wheeler asked his advice with regard to that tree,—whether he could do better than lay the axe at its root. F. told him that he had seen an ash in the old country which was in the same condition, and is a tenderer tree than an "elum," preserved by being filled up, and with masonry, and then cemented over. So, soon after, the mason was set to work upon it under his directions, Flood having scraped out all the rotten wood first with a hoe. The cavity was full three feet wide and eight or ten high commencing at the ground. The mason had covered the bricks and rounded off with mortar, which he had scored with his trowel so that [one] did not observe but it was bark. It seemed an admirable plan, and not only improved the appearance but the strength and durability of the tree.

Not till June can the grass be said to be waving in the fields. When the frogs dream, and the grass waves, and the buttercups toss their heads, and the heat disposes to bathe in the ponds and streams, then is summer begun.

Conantum pool looking south across pasture, Concord, Massachusetts

Wild roses, Concord, Massachusetts

HERE are many wild roses northeast of Trillium Woods. We are liable to underrate this flower on account of its commonness. Is it not the queen of our flowers? How ample and high-colored its petals, glancing half concealed from its own green bowers! There is a certain noble and delicate civility about it,—not wildness. It is properly the type of the *Rosaceæ*, or flowers among others of most wholesome fruits. It is at home in the garden, as readily cultivated as apples. It is the pride of June. In summing up its attractions I should mention its rich color, size, and form, the rare beauty of its bud, its fine fragrance, and the beauty of the entire shrub, not to mention the almost innumerable varieties it runs into. I bring home the buds ready to expand, put them in a pitcher of water, and the next morning they open and fill my chamber with fragrance. This, found in the wilderness, must have reminded the Pilgrim of home.

HAVING NOTICED the pine pollen washed up on the shore of three or four ponds in the woods lately and at Ripple Lake, a dozen rods from the nearest pine, also having seen the pollen carried off visibly half a dozen rods from a pitch pine which I had jarred, and rising all the while when there was very little wind, it suggested to me that the air must be full of this fine dust at this season, that it must be carried to great distances, when dry, and falling at night perhaps, or with a change in the atmosphere, its presence might be detected remote from pines by examining the edges of pretty large bodies of water, where it would be collected to one side by the wind and waves from a large area.

So I thought over all the small ponds in the township in order to select one or more most remote from the woods or pines, whose shores I might examine and so test my theory. I could think of none more favorable than this little pond only four rods in diameter, a watering-place in John Brown's pasture, which has but few pads in it. It is a small round pond at the bottom of a hollow in the midst of a perfectly bare, dry pasture. The nearest wood of any kind is just thirty-nine rods distant northward, and across a road from the edge of the pond. Any other wood in other directions is five or six times as far. I knew it was a bad time to try my experiment,—just after such heavy rains and when the pines are effete,—a little too late. The wind was now blowing quite strong from the northeast, whereas all the pollen that

I had seen hitherto had been collected on the northeast sides of ponds by a southwest wind. I approached the pond from the northeast and, looking over it and carefully along the shore there, could detect no pollen. I then proceeded to walk round it, but still could detect none. I then said to myself, If there was any here before the rain and northeast wind, it must have been on the northeast side and then have been washed over and now up high quite at or on the shore. I looked there carefully, stooping down, and was gratified to find, after all, a distinct yellow line of pollen dust about half an inch in width—or washing off to two or three times that width—quite on the edge, and some dead twigs which I took up from the wet shore were completely coated with

it, as with sulphur. This yellow line reached half a rod along the southwest side, and I then detected a little of the dust slightly graying the surface for two or three feet out there. (Many little snow(?)-fleas on it.)

When I thought I had failed, I was much pleased to detect, after all, this distinct yellow line, revealing unmistakably the presence of pines in the neighborhood and thus confirming my theory. As chemists detect the presence of ozone in the atmosphere by exposing to it a delicately prepared paper, so the lakes detect for us thus the presence of the pine pollen in the atmosphere. They are our *pollinometers*. How much of this invisible dust must be floating in the atmosphere, and be inhaled and drunk by us at this season!!

Pitch pine, Concord, Massachusetts

Rose hip of sweet briar, Concord, Massachusetts

WE NOW have roses on the land and lilies on the water,—both land and water have done their best,—now *just* after the longest day. Nature says, "You behold the utmost I can do." And the young women carry their finest roses on the other hand. Roses and lilies. The floral days. The red rose, with the intense color of many suns concentrated, spreads its tender petals perfectly fair, its flower not to be overlooked, modest yet queenly, on the edges of shady copses and meadows, against its green leaves, surrounded by blushing buds, of perfect form; not only beautiful, but rightfully commanding attention; unspoiled by the admiration of gazers. And the water-lily floats on the smooth surface of slow waters, amid rounded shields of leaves, bucklers, red beneath, which simulate a green field, perfuming the air. Each instantly the prey of the spoiler,—the rose-bug and water-insects. How transitory the perfect beauty of the rose and lily! The highest, intensest color belongs to the land, the purest, perchance, to the water.

THE BLUE FLAG (*Iris versicolor*). Its buds are a dark indigo-blue tip beyond the green calyx. It is rich but hardly delicate and simple enough; a very handsome sword-shaped leaf. The blue-eyed grass is one of the most beautiful of flowers. It might have been famous from Proserpine down. It will bear to be praised by poets. The blue flag, notwithstanding its rich furniture, its fringed recurved parasols over its anthers, and its variously streaked and odored petals, is loose and coarse in its habit. How completely all character is expressed by flowers! This is a little too showy and gaudy, like some women's bonnets. Yet it belongs to the meadow and ornaments as much.

Blue flag, Mt. Monadnock, New Hampshire

Landing on Tall's Island, I perceive a sour scent from the wilted leaves and scraps of leaves which were blown off yesterday and strew the ground in all woods.

Just within the edge of the wood there, I see a small painted turtle on its back, with its head stretched out as if to turn over. Surprised by the sight, I stooped to investigate the cause. It drew in its head at once, but I noticed that its shell was partially empty. I could see through it from side to side as it lay, its entrails having been extracted through large openings just before the hind legs. The dead leaves were flattened for a foot over, where it had been operated on, and were a little bloody. Its paunch lay on the leaves, and contained much vegetable matter,—old cranberry leaves, etc. Judging by the striæ, it was not more than five or six years old,—or four or five. Its fore parts were quite alive, its hind legs apparently dead, its inwards gone; apparently its spine perfect. The flies had entered it in numbers. What creature could have done this which it would be difficult for a man to do? I thought of a skunk, weazel, mink, but I do not believe that they could have got their snouts into so small a space as that in front of the hind legs between the shells. The hind legs themselves had not been injured nor the shell scratched. I thought it most likely that it was done by some bird of the heron kind which has a long and powerful bill. And probably this accounts for the many dead turtles which I have found and thought died from disease. Such is Nature, who gave one creature a taste or yearning for another's entrails as its favorite tidbit!! I thought the more of a bird, for, just as we were shoving away from this isle, I heard a sound just like a small dog barking hoarsely, and, looking up, saw it was made by a bittern (*Ardea minor*), a pair of which were flapping over the meadows and probably had a nest in some tussock thereabouts. No wonder the turtle is wary, for, notwithstanding its horny shell, when it comes forth to lay its eggs it runs the risk of having its entrails plucked out. That is the reason that the box turtle, which lives on the land, is made to shut itself up entirely within the shell, and I suspect that the mud tortoise only comes forth by night. What need the turtle has of some horny shield over those tender parts and avenues to its entrails! I saw several of these painted turtles dead on the bottom.

Dead painted turtle, Concord, Massachusetts

Clover field, crest of Fair Haven Hill, Concord, Massachusetts

THERE IS a great deal of white clover this year. In many fields where there has been no clover seed sown for many years at least, it is more abundant than the red, and the heads are nearly as large. Also pastures which are close cropped, and where I think there was little or no clover last year, are spotted white with a humbler growth. And everywhere, by roadsides, garden borders, etc., even where the sward is trodden hard, the small white heads on short stems are sprinkled everywhere As this is the season for the swarming of bees, and this clover is very attractive to them, it is probably the more difficult to secure them; at any rate it is the more important to secure their services now that they can make honey so fast. It is an interesting inquiry why this year is so favorable to the growth of clover!

Each FARMER values his spring and takes pride in it. He is inclined to think it the coldest in the neighborhood.

Each one is the source of a streamlet which finds its way into the river, though possibly one or two of them may dry up some seasons. Only one to my knowledge visibly bubbles up,—or did before interfered with,—*viz.* the Boiling Spring, which is the coldest. This would indicate that its reservoir is still higher considerably and deep within the hill. You commonly see the water coming in more or less copiously through the gravel on the upper side, sometimes from under a rock in a considerable stream and with a tinkling sound.

The coldest, as I notice, have the clearest and most crystalline or Walden-Pond-like look.

Henry Shattuck's two were of the same temperature, though one was in the open meadow at the head of a ditch, and the other in the bank and covered or boxed over. This shows that they come at once from a considerable depth in the earth and have no time to be warmed before they flow off. A rail standing on its end in one of his ditches was almost concealed, so deep is the mud in his meadow. He pointed out two or three in his ditches "as big as your body" and of unknown depth.

No. 1 is at the head of them all, and no doubt was used by the Indians. It is used by the Fitchburg Railroad for their locomotives. No. 2 was made in cutting for the railroad, and is used by the track-repairers. Some are far away and only used by hunters and walkers and berry-pickers. Some are used in haying-time only. Some are so cold and clear, and so near withal, as to be used daily by some family, who "turn up their noses" at the well. Others, as Dugan's, are instead of the well. One, as Wheeler's, has had five hundred dollars expended on it. No. 6 was found by Hosmer when he built his dam, and he imagines that it has medicinal properties, and used accordingly to come to drink at it often, though half a mile from his house. Some will have a broken tumbler hid in the grass near, or a rusty dipper hung on a twig near by. Others, again, drink through some hollow weed's stem. None are too cold for the *Rana fontinalis*, which will hardly make room for your face when you stoop to drink. Some are only known to myself and friends, and I clear them out annually.

I suspect that most of them never freeze entirely over.

Brister's Spring, Concord, Massachusetts

"Asa Gray Spring" (Minot Pratt's), Concord, Massachusetts

Cows in pasture, old Tarbell place, Concord, Massachusetts

Roses are in their prime now, growing amid huckleberry bushes, ferns, and sweet-ferns, especially about some dry pond-hole; some paler, some more red. Methinks they must have bloomed in vain while only wild men roamed, yet now they only adorn these cows' pasture.

How well-behaved are cows! When they approach me reclining in the shade, from curiosity, or to receive a whisp of grass, or to share the shade, or to lick the dog held up, like a calf,—though just now they ran at him to toss him,— they do not obtrude. Their company is acceptable, for they can endure the longest pause; they have not got to be entertained. They occupy the most eligible lots in the town. I love to see some pure white about them; they suggest the more neatness.

THE WIND exposes the red under sides of the white lily pads. This is one of the aspects of the river now. The bud-bearing stem of this plant is a little larger, but otherwise like the leaf-stem, and coming like it directly from the long, large root. It is interesting to pull up the lily root with flowers and leaves attached and see how it sends its buds upward to the light and air to expand and flower in another element. How interesting the bud's progress from the water to the air! So many of these stems are leaf-bearing, and so many flower-bearing. Then consider how defended these plants against drought, at the bottom of the water, at most their leaves and flowers floating on its surface. How much mud and water are required to support their vitality! It is pleasant to remember those quiet Sabbath mornings by remote stagnant rivers and ponds, when pure white water-lilies, just expanded, not yet infested by insects, float on the waveless water and perfume the atmosphere. Nature never appears more serene and innocent and fragrant. A hundred white lilies, open to the sun, rest on the surface smooth as oil amid their pads, while devil's-needles are glancing over them. It requires some skill so to pull a lily as to get a long stem. The great yellow lily, the spatterdock, expresses well the fertility of the river. . . .

June 30. Nature must be viewed humanly to be viewed at all; that is, her scenes must be associated with humane affections, such as are associated with one's native place, for instance. She is most significant to a lover. A lover of Nature is preëminently a lover of man. If I have no friend, what is Nature to me? She ceases to be morally significant.

Pond lilies in Fair Haven Bay, Concord, Massachusetts

WHAT shall we do with a man who is afraid of the woods, their solitude and darkness? What salvation is there for him? God is silent and mysterious.

Some of our richest days are those in which no sun shines outwardly, but so much the more a sun shines inwardly. I love nature, I love the landscape, because it is so sincere. It never cheats me. It never jests. It is cheerfully, musically earnest. I lie and relie [*sic*] on the earth.

Land where the wood has been cut off and is just beginning to come up again is called sprout land.

The sweet-scented life-everlasting has not lost its scent yet, but smells like the balm of the fields.

The partridge-berry leaves checker the ground on the side of moist hillsides in the woods. Are *they* not properly called *checker*-berries?

The era of wild apples will soon be over. I wander through old orchards of great extent, now all gone to decay, all of native fruit which for the most part went to the cider-mill. But since the temperance reform and the general introduction of grafted fruit, no wild apples, such as I see everywhere in deserted pastures, and where the woods have grown up among them, are set out. I fear that he who walks over these hills a century hence will not know the pleasure of knocking off wild apples. Ah, poor man! there are many pleasures which he will be debarred from! Notwithstanding the prevalence of the Baldwin and the Porter. I doubt if as extensive orchards set out to-day in this town as there were a century ago, when these vast straggling cider-orchards were planted. Men stuck in a tree then by every wall-side and let it take its chance. I see nobody planting trees to-day in such out of the way places, along almost every road and lane and wall-side, and at the bottom of dells in the wood. Now that they have grafted trees and pay a price for them, they collect them into a plot by their houses and fence them in.

My Journal should be the record of my love. I would write in it only of the things I love, my affection for any aspect of the world, what I love to think of. I have no more distinctness or pointedness in my yearnings than an expanding bud, which does indeed point to flower and fruit, to summer and autumn, but is aware of the warm sun and spring influence only. I feel ripe for something, yet do nothing, can't discover what that thing is. I feel fertile merely. It is seedtime with me. I have lain fallow long enough.

Notwithstanding a sense of unworthiness which possesses me, not without reason, notwithstanding that I regard myself as a good deal of a scamp, yet for the most part the spirit of the universe is unaccountably kind to me, and I enjoy perhaps an unusual share of happiness. Yet I question sometimes if there is not some settlement to come.

Partridge-berry, Concord, Massachusetts

Field of rye, Concord, Massachusetts

Here are some rich rye-fields waving over all the land, their heads nodding in the evening breeze with an apparently alternating motion; *i.e.* they do not all bend at once by ranks, but separately, and hence this agreeable alternation. How rich a sight this cereal fruit, now yellow for the cradle,—*flavus!* It is an impenetrable phalanx. I walk for half a mile beside these Macedonians, looking in vain for an opening. There is no Arnold Winkelried to gather these spear-heads upon his breast and make an opening for me. This is food for man. The earth labors not in vain; it is bearing its burden. The yellow, waving, rustling rye extends far up and over the hills on either side, a kind of pinafore to nature, leaving only a narrow and dark passage at the bottom of a deep ravine. How rankly it has grown! How it hastes to maturity! I discover that there is such a goddess as Ceres. These long grain-fields which you must respect,—must go round,—occupying the ground like an army. The small trees and shrubs seen dimly in its midst are overwhelmed by the grain as by an inundation. They are seen only as indistinct forms of bushes and green leaves mixed with the yellow stalks. There are certain crops which give me the idea of bounty, of the *Alma Natura*. They are the grains. Potatoes do not so fill the lap of earth. This rye excludes everything else and takes possession of the soil. The farmer says, "Next year I will raise a crop of rye;" and he proceeds to clear away the brush, and either plows it, or, if it is too uneven or stony, burns and harrows it only, and scatters the seed with faith. And all winter the earth keeps his secret,—unless it did leak out somewhat in the fall,—and in the spring this early green on the hillsides betrays him. When I see this luxuriant crop spreading far and wide in spite of rock and bushes and unevenness of ground, I cannot help thinking that it must have been unexpected by the farmer himself, and regarded by him as a lucky accident for which to thank fortune. This, to reward a transient faith, the gods had given. As if he must have forgotten that he did it, until he saw the waving grain inviting his sickle.

THE loudest sound that burdens here the breeze
Is the wood's whisper; 't is, when we choose to list,
Audible sound, and when we list not,
It is calm profound. Tongues were provided
But to vex the ear with superficial thoughts.
When deeper thoughts upswell, the jarring discord
Of harsh speech is hushed, and senses seem
As little as may be to share the ecstasy.

Emerson's Cliff, "My Garden", Concord, Massachusetts

Afternoons, I sounded the Assabet as far up as the stone bridge....

A considerable island has been formed there, at least three feet and a half above low water, composed of sand, and, two or three rods lower, are deposited the stones, generally larger than a hen's egg, without sand, forming bars and islands quite distinct from the former. This is much the swiftest place on the stream thus far and deeper than any for twenty-five miles of [the] other stream, and consequently there is a great eddy, where I see cakes of ice go round and round in the spring, and, as usual, the shoal water and islands formed by the ruins of the bank and of the bottom are close by. As usual, the shoal water is produced by the rapidity of the current close by.

The sand and gravel are deposited chiefly in the immediate neighborhood of the swiftest water, the swift water producing an eddy. Hence, apparently, the sandy islands at the junction of the rivers, the sand-bar at the swift place on the Assabet, etc. Contract the stream and make it swift, and you will wear a deep hole and make sand-bars and islands below.

Island at "Eddy Bend," Concord, Massachusetts

Old Conantum lilacs and wood road, Concord, Massachusetts

The forenoon is fuller of light. The butterflies on the flowers look like other and frequently larger flowers themselves. Now I yearn for one of those old, meandering, dry, uninhabited roads, which lead away from towns, which lead us away from temptation, which conduct to the outside of earth, over its uppermost crust; where you may forget in what country you are travelling; where no farmer can complain that you are treading down his grass, no gentleman who has recently constructed a seat in the country that you are trespassing; on which you can go off at half-cock and wave adieu to the village; along which you may travel like a pilgrim, going nowhither; where travellers are not too often to be met; where my spirit is free; where the walls and fences are not cared for; where your head is more in heaven than your feet are on earth; which have long reaches where you can see the approaching traveller half a mile off and be prepared for him; not so luxuriant a soil as to attract men; some root and stump fences which do not need attention; where travellers have no occasion to stop, but pass along and leave you to your thoughts; where it makes no odds which way you face, whether you are going or coming, whether it is morning or evening, mid-noon or midnight; where earth is cheap enough by being public; where you can walk and think with least obstruction, there being nothing to measure progress by; where you can pace when your breast is full, and cherish your moodiness; where you are not in false relations with men, are not dining nor conversing with them; by which you may go to the uttermost parts of the earth. It is wide enough, wide as the thoughts it allows to visit you.

. . .

A thinker's weight is in his thought, not in his tread: when he thinks freely, his body weighs nothing. He cannot tread down your grass, farmers.

THE BEST SHOW of lilies is on the west side of the bay, in Cyrus Hosmer's meadow, above the willow-row. Many of them are not open at 10 o'clock A.M. I noticed one with the sepals perfectly spread flat on the water, but the petals still held together in a sharp cone, being held by the concave, slightly hooked points. Touching this with an oar, it opens quickly with a spring. The same with many others, whose sepals were less spread. Under the influence of the light and warmth, the petals elevate or expand themselves in the middle, becoming more and more convex, till at last, being released at their overlapping points, they spring open and quickly spread themselves equally, revealing their yellow stamens. How satisfactory is the fragrance of this flower! It is the emblem of purity. It reminds me of a young country maiden. It is just so simple and unproved. Wholesome as the odor of the cow. It is not a highly refined odor, but merely a fresh youthful morning sweetness. It is merely the unalloyed sweetness of the earth and the water; a fair opportunity and field for life; like its petals, uncolored by any experience; a simple maiden on her way to school, her face surrounded by a white ruff. But how quickly it becomes the prey of insects!

Pond lily

Skunk cabbage at Clamshell Bank, Concord, Massachusetts

You see now in the meadows where the mower's scythe has cut in two the great oval and already black fruit of the skunk-cabbage, rough as a nutmeg-grater, exposing its numerous nuts. I had quite forgotten the promise of this earliest spring flower, which, deep in the grass which has sprung up around it, its own leaves for the most part decayed, unremembered by us, has been steadily maturing its fruit. How far we have wandered, in our thoughts at least, since we heard the bee humming in its spathe! I can hardly recall or believe now that for every such black and rather unsightly (?) capsule there was a pretty freckled horn which attracted our attention in the spring. However, most of them lie so low that they escape or are not touched by the scythe.[1]

[1] My friends can rarely guess what fruit it is, but think of pine-apples and the like. After lying in the house a week, and being wilted and softened, on breaking it open it has an agreeable sweetish scent, perchance like a banana, and suggests that it may be edible. But a long while after slightly tasting it, it bites my palate.

Concentric lichens on bark, Mt. Monadnock, New Hampshire

The apparently common green and white cladonias, together with yet whiter stereocaulon, grew all over the flat rocks in profusion, and the apparently common greenish rock lichen . . . grew concentricwise in large circles on the slopes of rocks also, not to mention the common small umbilicaria . . . of one or two kinds which covered the brows and angles of the rocks.

Spray of yew in fruit, Bridgton, Maine

A M SURPRISED to find the yew with ripe fruit (how long?),—though there is a little still small and green,—where I had not detected fertile flowers. It fruits very sparingly, the berries growing singly here and there, on last year's wood, and hence four to six inches below the extremities of the upturned twigs. It is the most surprising berry that we have: first, since it is borne by an evergreen, hemlock-like bush with which we do not associate a soft and bright-colored berry, and hence its deep scarlet contrasts the more strangely with the pure, dark evergreen needles; and secondly, because of its form, so like art, and which could be easily imitated in wax, a very thick scarlet cup or mortar with a dark-purple(?) bead set at the bottom. My neighbors are not prepared to believe that such a berry grows in Concord.

Lee's Bridge from road, Concord, Massachusetts

THE WILLOW REACH by Lee's Bridge has been stripped for powder. None escapes. This morning, hearing a cart, I looked out and saw George Dugan going by with a horse-load of his willow toward Acton powder-mills, which I had seen in piles by the turnpike. Every traveller has just as particular an errand which I might likewise chance to be privy to.

A DOG-DAY, comfortably cloudy and cool as well as still. The river meadows, where no mowing, have a yellowish and autumnal look, especially the wool-grass. I see large flocks of bobolinks on the Union Turnpike. Are the darker ones with some yellowish (?) on side heads young red-wings or male bobolinks changing? Forded the Assabet at the bathing-place. Saw carrion-flower berries just begun to turn; say in a day or two. Panicled cornel berries on College Road. Many of the trees in Barrett's orchard on Annur-snack touch the ground all around like a dish cover, weighed down with fruit, and the branches are no thicker over head than around. Is not this the best form for an apple tree,— a hollow hemisphere nearly resting on the earth, the branches equally dispersed over the superficies, and light and air equally admitted? Hills and pastures are now dry and slippery. They seem as completely russet as in winter. I associate the mist of this dog-day with the burning of meadows. Crossed from top of Annursnack to top of Strawberry Hill, past a pigeon-bed. Measured the great chestnut. At about seven feet from ground, the smallest place I could find, it is 14-3/4 feet in circumference; at six feet from ground, 15-1/12 feet in circumference; at five feet, 15-4/12; at one foot from ground not including some bulgings, 22 feet in circumference. It branches first at about nine feet from ground. The top has some dead limbs and is not large in proportion to trunk. There are great furrows in the bark.

Great chestnut tree near Herman's Chestnut House, Wayland, Massachusetts

To GOWING'S SWAMP and Hadlock Meadows.

I improve the dry weather to examine the middle of
Gowing's Swamp. There is in the middle an open pool,
twenty or thirty feet in diameter, nearly full of sphagnum
and green froth on the surface (frog-spittle), and what other
plants I could not see on account of the danger in standing
on the quaking ground; then a dense border, a rod or more
wide, of a peculiar rush (?), with clusters of seed-vessels,
three together, now going to seed, a yellow green, forming
an abrupt edge next the water, this on a dense bed of
quaking sphagnum, in which I sink eighteen inches in water,
upheld by its matted roots, where I fear to break through.

Pond hole in Gowing's Swamp, Concord, Massachusetts

On this the spatulate sundew abounds. This is marked by the paths of muskrats, which also extend through the green froth of the pool. Next comes, half a dozen rods wide, a dense bed of *Andromeda calyculata,*—the *A. Polifolia* mingled with it,—the rusty cotton-grass, cranberries,—the common and also *V. Oxycoccus,*—pitcher-plants, sedges, and a few young spruce and larch here and there,—all on sphagnum, which forms little hillocks about the stems of the andromeda. Then ferns, now yellowing, high blueberry bushes, etc., etc., etc.,—or the bushy and main body of the swamp, under which the sphagnum is now dry and white.

Tʜᴇ ʀɪᴠᴇʀ is eight and one twelfth feet below top of truss. Add eight and a half inches for its greatest height this year, and you have eight feet nine and a half inches for the difference. It is apparently as low now as the first week in July. That is, those are the limits of our river's expansibility; so much it may swell. Of course, the water now in it is but a small fraction of that which it contains in the highest freshets, for this additional eight and nine twelfths feet is much more than its present average depth, half as much again perhaps, beside averaging eight or ten times its present width.

To CLINTONIA SWAMP and Cardinal Ditch.

Unusually cold last night.

Goodyera pubescens, rattlesnake-plantain, is apparently a *little* past its prime. It is very abundant on Clintonia Swamp hillside, quite erect, with its white spike eight to ten inches high on the sloping hillside, the lower half or more turning brown, but the beautifully reticulated leaves which pave the moist shady hillside about its base are the chief attraction. These oval leaves, perfectly smooth like velvet to the touch, about one inch long, have a broad white midrib and four to six longitudinal white veins, very prettily and thickly connected by other conspicuous white veins transversely and irregularly, all on a dark rich green ground. Is it not the prettiest leaf that paves the forest floor? As a cultivated exotic it would attract great attention for its leaf. Many of the leaves are eaten. Is it by partridges? It is a leaf of firm texture, not apt to be partially eaten by insects or decayed, and does not soon wilt. So unsoiled and undecayed. It might be imitated on carpets and rugs. Some old withered stems of last year still stand.

Leaves of rattlesnake plantain

Field of mulleins and St. Johnsworts, Concord, Massachusetts

Walked along the Clamshell bank after sundown. A cloudy sky. The heads of the grass in the pasture behind Dennis's have a reddish cast, but another grass, with a lighter-colored stem and leaves, on the higher parts of the field gives a yellowish tinge to those parts, as if they reflected a misty sunlight. Even much later in the night these light spots were distinguishable. I am struck by the cool, juicy, pickled-cucumber green of the potato-fields now. How lusty these vines look! The pasture naturally exhibits at this season no such living green as the cultivated fields. I perceive that flower of the lowlands now, with a peculiar leaf and conspicuous white umbels.

Here are mulleins covering a field (the Clamshell field) where three years [ago] were none noticeable, but a smooth uninterrupted pasture sod. Two years ago it was plowed for the first time for many years, and millet and corn and potatoes planted, and now *where the millet grew* these mulleins have sprung up. Who can write the history of these fields? The millet does not perpetuate itself, but the few seeds of the mullein, which perchance were brought here with it, are still multiplying the race.

The thick heads of the yellow dock warn me of the lapse of time.

Butterflies on pasture thistle, Bridgton, Maine

The pasture thistle, though past its prime, is quite common, and almost every flower (*i.e.* thistle), wherever you meet with it, has one or more bumblebees on it, clambering over its mass of florets. One such bee which I disturb has much ado before he can rise from the grass and get under weigh, as if he were too heavily laden, and at last he flies but low. Now that flowers are rarer, almost every one of whatever species has bees or butterflies upon it.

THERE IS a little grove in a swampy place in Conantum where some rare things grow,—several bass trees, two kinds of ash, sassafras, maidenhair fern, the white-berried plant (ivory?), etc., etc., and the sweet viburnum (?) in the hedge near by.

Dicksonia fern, Conantum, Concord, Massachusetts

Having with some difficulty discovered the trail again, we kept up the south side of the West Branch, or main river, passing by some rapids called Rock-Ebeeme, the roar of which we heard through the woods, and, shortly after, in the thickest of the wood, some empty loggers' camps, still new, which were occupied the previous winter. Though we saw a few more afterwards, I will make one account serve for all. These were such houses as the lumberers of Maine spend the winter in, in the wilderness. There were the camps and the hovels for the cattle, hardly distinguishable, except that the latter had no chimney. These camps were about twenty feet long by fifteen wide, built of logs,—hemlock, cedar, spruce or yellow birch—one kind alone, or all together, with the bark on; two or three large ones first, one directly above another, and notched together at the ends, to the height of three or four feet, then of smaller logs resting upon transverse ones at the ends, each of the last successively shorter than the other, to form the roof. The chimney was an oblong square hole in the middle, three or four feet in diameter, with a fence of logs as high as the ridge. The interstices were filled with moss, and the roof was shingled with long and handsome splints of cedar, or spruce, or pine, rifted with a sledge and cleaver. The fireplace, the most important place of all, was in shape and size like the chimney, and directly under it, defined by a log fence or fender on the ground, and a heap of ashes, a foot or two deep within, with solid benches of split logs running round it. Here the fire usually melts the snow, and dries the rain before it can descend to quench it. The faded beds of arbor-vitæ leaves extended under the eaves on either hand. There was the place for the water-pail, pork-barrel, and wash-basin, and generally a dingy pack of cards left on a log. Usually a good deal of whittling was expended on the latch, which was made of wood, in the form of an iron one. These houses are made comfortable by the huge fires, which can be afforded night and day. Usually the scenery about them is drear and savage enough; and the logger's camp is as completely in the woods as a fungus at the foot of a pine in a swamp; no outlook but to the sky overhead; no more clearing than is made by cutting down the trees of which it is built, and those which are necessary for fuel. If only it be well sheltered and convenient to his work, and near a spring, he wastes no thought on the prospect. They are very proper forest houses, the stems of the trees collected together and piled up around a man to keep out wind and rain,—made of living green logs, hanging with moss and lichen, and with the curls and fringes of the yellow birch bark, and dripping with resin, fresh and moist, and redolent of swampy odors, with that sort of vigor and perennialness even about them that toadstools suggest. The logger's fare consists of tea, molasses, flour, pork (sometimes beef), and beans. A great proportion of the beans raised in Massachusetts find their market here. On expeditions it is only hard bread and pork, often raw, slice upon slice, with tea or water, as the case may be.

Marnhill's Camp, Squaw Pond, Greenville, Maine

Squaw Mountain and edge of spruce woods, Greenville, Maine

THIS WAS an interesting botanical locality for one coming from the south to commence with; for many plants which are rather rare, and one or two which are not found at all, in the eastern part of Massachusetts, grew abundantly between the rails,—as Labrador-tea, *Kalmia glauca*, Canada blueberry (which was still in fruit, and a second time in bloom), *Clintonia* and *Linnæa borealis*, which last a lumberer called *moxon*, creeping snowberry, painted trillium, large-flowered bellwort, etc. I fancied that the *Aster Radula, Diplopappus umbellatus, Solidago lanceolata*, red trumpet-weed, and many others which were conspicuously in bloom on the shore of the lake and on the carry, had a peculiarly wild and primitive look there. The spruce and fir trees crowded to the track on each side to welcome us, the arbor-vitæ, with its changing leaves, prompted us to make haste, and the sight of the canoe birch gave us spirits to do so. Sometimes an evergreen just fallen lay across the track with its rich burden of cones, looking, still, fuller of life than our trees in the most favorable positions. You did not

expect to find such *spruce* trees in the wild woods, but they evidently attend to their toilets each morning even there. Through such a front yard did we enter that wilderness.

PADDLING along the eastern side of the lake in the still of the morning, we soon saw a few sheldrakes, which the Indian called *Shecorways*, and some peetweets, *Naramekechus*, on the rocky shore; we also saw and heard loons, *Medawisla*, which he said was a sign of wind. It was inspiriting to hear the regular dip of the paddles, as if they were our fins or flippers, and to realize that we were at length fairly embarked. We who had felt strangely as stage-passengers and tavern-lodgers were suddenly naturalized there and presented with the freedom of the lakes and the woods. Having passed the small rocky isles within two or three miles of the foot of the lake, we had a short consultation respecting our course, and inclined to the western shore for the sake of its lee; for otherwise, if the wind should rise, it would be impossible for us to reach Mount Kineo, which is about midway up the lake on the east side, but at its narrowest part, where probably we could recross if we took the western side. The wind is the chief obstacle to crossing the lakes, especially in so small a canoe. The Indian remarked several times that he did not like to cross the lakes "in littlum canoe," but nevertheless, "just as we say, it made no odds to him." He sometimes took a straight course up the middle of the lake between Sugar and Deer islands, when there was no wind.

Measured on the map, Moosehead Lake is twelve miles wide at the widest place, and thirty miles long in a direct line, but longer as it lies. The captain of the steamer called it thirty-eight miles as he steered. We should probably go about forty. The Indian said that it was called "*Mspame*, because large water." Squaw Mountain rose darkly on our left, near the outlet of the Kennebec, and what the Indian called Spencer Bay Mountain, on the east, and already we saw Mount Kineo before us in the north.

Paddling near the shore, we frequently heard the *pe-pe* of the olive-sided flycatcher, also the wood pewee, and the kingfisher, thus early in the morning. The Indian reminding us that he could not work without eating, we stopped to breakfast on the main shore, southwest of Deer Island, at a spot where the *Mimulus ringens* grew abundantly. We took out our bags, and the Indian made a fire under a very large bleached log, using white pine bark from a stump, though he said that hemlock was better, and kindling with canoe birch bark. Our table was a large piece of freshly peeled birch bark, laid wrong side up, and our breakfast consisted of hard-bread, fried pork, and strong coffee, well sweetened, in which we did not miss the milk.

While we were getting breakfast, a brood of twelve black dippers, half grown, came paddling by within three or four rods, not at all alarmed; and they loitered about as long as we stayed, now huddled close together, within a circle of eighteen inches in diameter, now moving off in a long line, very cunningly. Yet they bore a certain proportion to the great Moosehead Lake on whose bosom they floated, and I felt as if they were under its protection.

Squaw Mountain and lake from Blair's, Greenville, Maine

String of fish from Moose Pond, Bridgton, Maine

BUT THERE is the rough voice of Uncle George, who commands at the frying-pan, to send over what you've got, and then you may stay till morning. The pork sizzles, and cries for fish. Luckily for the foolish race, and this particularly foolish generation of trout, the night shut down at last, not a little deepened by the dark side of Ktaadn, which, like a permanent shadow, reared itself from the eastern bank. Lescarbot, writing in 1609, tells us that the Sieur Champdoré, who, with one of the people of the Sieur de Monts, ascended some fifty leagues up the St. John in 1608, found the fish so plenty, "qu'en mettant la chaudière sur le feu ils en avoient pris suffisamment pour eux dìsner avant que l'eau fust chaude." Their descendants here are no less numerous.

WHAT IS most striking in the Maine wilderness is the continuousness of the forest, with fewer open intervals or glades than you had imagined. Except the few burnt lands, the narrow intervals on the rivers, the bare tops of the high mountains, and the lakes and streams, the forest is uninterrupted. It is even more grim and wild than you had anticipated, a damp and intricate wilderness, in the spring everywhere wet and miry. The aspect of the country, indeed, is universally stern and savage, excepting the distant views of the forest from hills, and the lake prospects, which are mild and civilizing in a degree. The lakes are something which you are unprepared for: they lie up so high, exposed to the light, and the forest is diminished to a fine fringe on their edges, with here and there a blue mountain, like amethyst jewels set around some jewel of the first water,—so anterior, so superior, to all the changes that are to take place on their shores, even now civil and refined, and fair as they can ever be. These are not the artificial forests of an English king,—a royal preserve merely. Here prevail no forest laws but those of nature. The aborigines have never been dispossessed, nor nature disforested.

It is a country full of evergreen trees, of mossy silver birches and watery maples, the ground dotted with insipid small, red berries, and strewn with damp and moss-grown rocks,—a country diversified with innumerable lakes and rapid streams, peopled with trout and various species of *leucisci*, with salmon, shad, and pickerel, and other fishes; the forest resounding at rare intervals with the note of the chickadee, the blue jay, and the woodpecker, the scream of the fish hawk and the eagle, the laugh of the loon, and the whistle of ducks along the solitary streams; at night, with the hooting of owls and howling of wolves; in summer, swarming with myriads of black flies and mosquitoes, more formidable than wolves to the white man. Such is the home of the moose, the bear, the caribou, the wolf, the beaver, and the Indian. Who shall describe the inexpressible tenderness and immortal life of the grim forest, where Nature, though it be midwinter, is ever in her spring, where the moss-grown and decaying trees are not old, but seem to enjoy a perpetual youth; and blissful, innocent Nature, like a serene infant, is too happy to make a noise, except by a few tinkling, lisping birds and trickling rills?

What a place to live, what a place to die and be buried in!

Wood interior on road up Benson Mt., Lake Onawa, Maine

Under an oak on the bank of the canal in Chelmsford. From Ball's Hill to Billerica meeting-house the river is a noble stream of water, flowing between gentle hills and occasional cliffs, and well wooded all the way. It can hardly be said to flow at all, but rests in the lap of the hills like a quiet lake. The boatmen call it a dead stream. For many long reaches you can see nothing to indicate that men inhabit its banks. Nature seems to hold a sabbath herself to-day,—a still warm sun on river and wood, and not breeze enough to ruffle the water. Cattle stand up to their bellies in the river, and you think Rembrandt should be here.

Ball's Hill opposite Brewster's cabin, Concord, Massachusetts

THIS IS the most glorious part of this day, the serenest, warmest, brightest part, and the most suggestive. Evening is fairer than morning. It is chaste eve, for it has sustained the trials of the day, but to the morning such praise was inapplicable. It is incense-breathing. Morning is full of promise and vigor. Evening is pensive. The serenity is far more remarkable to those who are on the water. That part of the sky just above the horizon seen reflected, apparently, some rods off from the boat is as light a blue as the actual, but it goes on deepening as your eye draws nearer to the boat, until, when you look directly down at the reflection of the zenith, it is lost in the blackness of the water. It passes through all degrees of dark blue, and the threatening aspect of a cloud is very much enhanced in the reflection. As I wish to be on the water at sunset, I let the boat float. I enjoy now the warmth of summer with some of the water prospect of spring. Looking westward, the surface of the water on the meadows in the sun has a slight dusty appearance, with clear black lines, as if some water nymph had written "slut" with her finger there.

A flock of half a dozen or more blue-winged teal, scared up down-stream behind me, as I was rowing, have circled round to reconnoitre and cross up-stream before me, quite close. I had seen another flock of ducks high in the air in the course of the day. Have ducks then begun to return?

I observe, on the willows on the east shore, the shadow of my boat and self and oars, upside down, and, I believe, it is joined to the same right side up, but the branches are so thin there that that shadow is not perfect. There goes a great bittern *plodding* home over the meadows at evening, to his perch on some tree by the shore. The rain has washed the leaves clean where he perches. There stands another in the meadow just like a stake, or the point of a stump or root. Its security was consulted both in its form and color. The latter is a sober brown, pale on the breast, as the less exposed side of a root might be; and its attitude is accidental, too, bent forward and *perfectly* motionless. Therefore there is no change in appearance but such as can be referred to the motion of the sailor.

American bittern on edge of boat, Concord, Massachusetts

ANOTHER FAIR DAY and wind northwest, but rather warmer. We kept along the road to Rockport, some two miles or more, to a "thundering big ledge" by the road, as a man called it; then turned off toward the south shore, at a house with two very large and old pear trees before it. Part of the house was built by a Witham, one of the first settlers, and the place or neighborhood used to be called "the Farms." Saw the *F. hyemalis* flitting along the walls, and it was cool enough for them on this cape. In a marsh by the shore, where was a very broad curving sandy beach, the shore of a cove, found the *Ranunculus Cymbalaria*, still in bloom, but mostly in fruit. *Glaux maritima* (?), nearly prostrate, with oblong leaves. *Triglochin palustris* in fruit.

An eleocharis, apparently marine, with lenticular fruit and a wrinkled mitre-shaped beak. *Spergularia rubra*, etc., samphire, etc.

The narrow road—where we followed it—wound about big boulders, past small, often *bevel*-roofed cottages where sometimes was a small flag flying for a vane. The number and variety of bevelled roofs on the Cape is surprising. Some are so nearly flat that they reminded me of the low brows of monkeys.

We had already seen a sort of bare rocky ridge, a bare boulder-covered back of the Cape, running northeasterly from Gloucester toward Rockport and for some three miles quite bare, the eastern extremity of the Cape being wooded. That would be a good place to walk.

Boulders on Dogtown Common, Gloucester, Massachusetts

Rockport well deserves its name,—several little rocky harbors protected by a breakwater, the houses at Rockport Village backing directly on the beach. At Folly Cove, a wild rocky point running north, covered with beach-grass. See now a mountain on the east of Agamenticus. Isles of Shoals too low to be seen. Probably land at Boar's Head, seen on the west of Agamenticus, and then the coast all the way from New Hampshire to Cape Ann plainly, New-buryport included and Plum Island. Hog Island looks like a high hill on the mainland.

Folly Cove, Rockport, Cape Ann, Massachusetts

BEHIND ONE HOUSE, an Indian had nearly finished one canoe and was just beginning another, outdoors. I looked very narrowly at the process and had already carefully examined and measured our birch. We asked this Indian his name. He answered readily and pleasantly, "My name is Old John Pennyweight." Said he got his bark at the head of Passadumkeag, fifty miles off. Took him two days to find one tree that was suitable; had to look very sharp to be sure the bark was not imperfect. But once he made two birches out of one tree. Took the bark off with a shovel made of rock maple, three or four inches wide. It took him a fortnight or three weeks to complete a canoe after he had got the materials ready. They sometimes made them of spruce bark, and also of skins, but they were not so good as birch. Boats of three hides were quicker made. This was the best time to get the birch bark. It would not come off in the winter. (I had heard Joe say of a certain canoe that it was made of summer bark.) They scrape all the inner bark off, and in the canoe the bark is wrong side outward.

He had the ribs of a canoe, all got out of cedar,—the first step in making a canoe, after materials [have been] brought together,—and each one shaped for the particular place it was to hold in the canoe. As both ends are alike, there will be two ribs alike. These two were placed close together, and the next in succession each way were placed next on each side, and thus tied up in bundles of fourteen to sixteen till all were made. In the bundle I examined, they were two and a half inches wide in the middle and narrowing to the ends. He would untie a bundle, take out the inmost, or longest, or several, and place them on their ends in a very large iron kettle of hot water over a fire, turning them from time to time. Then, taking one of the inmost or longest ones, he bent and shaped it with much labor over his knee, giving it with his eyes the shape it was to have in the canoe. It was then tied firmly and held in that shape with the reddish cedar bark. Sometimes he was obliged to tie a straight piece of wood on tangentwise to the rib, and, with a bark tie, draw out a side of the rib to that. Then each succeeding smaller rib in one half the bundle is forced into this. The first bundles of fourteen or sixteen making two bundles of steamed and bent and tied-up ribs; and thus all are left to dry in that shape.

I was sorry that I could not be there to witness the next step in making a canoe, for I was much struck by the *method* of this work, and the process deserves to be minutely described,—as much, at least, as most of the white man's arts, accounts of which now fill the journals. I do not know how the bark is made to hug so tightly the ribs, unless they are driven into place somewhat like a hoop. One of the next things must be to make the long, thin sheathing of cedar, less than half an inch thick, of pieces half the length of the birch, reaching each way close together beneath the ribs, and quite thin toward the edges of the canoe. However, I examined the canoe that was nearly done with minuteness. The edge or taffrail is composed first of two long strips of cedar, rather stout, one on each side. Four narrow hardwood (rock maple) cross-bars, artfully shaped so that no strength may be wasted, keep these apart, give firmness to the whole, and answer for seats. The ends of the ribs come up behind or outside this taffrail and are nailed to it with a single nail. Pennyweight said they formerly used wooden pegs. The edge of the bark is brought up level with this, and a very slender triangular cleat of cedar is nailed on over it and flush with the surface of the taffrail. Then there are ties of split white spruce bark (looking like split bamboo) through the bark, between the ribs, and around these two strips of cedar, and over the two strips one flat and thin strip covering the ties, making smooth work and coming out flush with the under strips. Thus the edge of the canoe is completed. Owing to the form of the canoe, there must be some seams near the edge on the sides about eighteen inches apart, and pieces of bark are put under them. The edges of the bark are carefully sewed together at the ends with the same spruce roots, and, in our canoe, a strip of canvas covered with pitch was laid (doubled) over the edge. They use rosin now, but pitch formerly. Canoe is nearly straight on bottom— straight in principle—and not so rounded the other way as is supposed. *Vide* this section in middle. The sides bulge out an inch or so beyond the rail. There is an additional piece of bark, four or five inches wide, along each side in the middle for four or five feet, for protection, and a similar protecting strip for eighteen inches on each side at the ends. The canoe rises about one foot in the last five or six feet. There is an oval piece of cedar for stiffness inside, within a foot of each end, and near this the ribs are bent short to breaking. Beyond there are not ribs, but sheaths and a small keel-like piece, and the hollow is filled with shavings. Lightness, above all, is studied in the construction. Nails and rosin were all the modern things I noticed. The maker used one of those curved knives, and worked very hard at bending the knees.

Thoreau's boat landing, Concord, Massachusetts

Joel Barrett's place (William Brewster's), Concord, Massachusetts

AGAIN AND AGAIN I am surprised to observe what an interval there is, in what is called civilized life, between the shell and the inhabitant of the shell,—what a disproportion there is between the life of man and his conveniences and luxuries. The house is neatly painted, has many apartments. You are shown into the sitting-room, where is a carpet and couch and mirror and splendidly bound Bible, daguerreotypes, ambrotypes, photographs of the whole family even, on the mantelpiece. One could live here more deliciously and improve his divine gifts better than in a cave surely. In the bright and costly saloon man will not be starving or freezing or contending with vermin surely, but he will be meditating a divine song or a heroic deed, or perfuming the atmosphere by the very breath of his natural and healthy existence. As the parlor is preferable to the cave, so will the life of its occupant be more godlike than that of the dweller in the cave. I called at such a house this afternoon, the house of one who in Europe would be called an operative. The woman was not in the third heavens, but in the third kitchen, as near the wood-shed or to outdoors and to the cave as she could instinctively get, for there she belonged,—a coarse scullion or wench, not one whit superior, but in fact inferior, to the squaw in a wigwam,—and the master of the house, where was he? He was drunk somewhere, on some mow or behind some stack, and I could not see him. He had been having a spree. If he had been as sober as he may be to-morrow, it would have been essentially the same; for refinement is not in him, it is only in his house,—in the appliances which he did not invent. So is it in the Fifth Avenue and all over the civilized world. There is nothing but confusion in our New England life. The hogs are in the parlor. This man and his wife—and how

many like them!—should have sucked their claws in some hole in a rock, or lurked like gypsies in the outbuildings of some diviner race. They've got into the wrong boxes; they rained down into these houses by mistake, as it is said to rain toads sometimes. They wear these advantages helter-skelter and without appreciating them, or to satisfy a vulgar taste, just as savages wear the dress of civilized men, just as that Indian chief walked the streets of New Orleans clad in nothing but a gaudy military coat which his Great Father had given him. Some philanthropists trust that the houses will civilize the inhabitants at last. The mass of men, just like savages, strive always after the outside, the clothes and finery of civilized life, the blue beads and tinsel and centre-tables. It is a wonder that any load ever gets moved, men are so prone to put the cart before the horse.

TO CLIFFS.

The dry grass yields a crisped sound to my feet. The white oak which appears to have made part of a hedge fence once, now standing in Hubbard's fence near the Corner road, where it stretches along horizontally, is (one of its arms, for it has one running each way) two and a half feet thick, with a sprout growing perpendicularly out of it eighteen inches in diameter. The corn-stalks standing in stacks, in long rows along the edges of the corn-fields, remind me of stacks of muskets.

FALL

THIS IS most serene autumn weather. The chirp of crickets may be heard at noon over all the land. As in summer they are heard only at nightfall, so now by their incessant chirp they usher in the evening of the year. The lively decay of autumn promises as infinite duration and freshness as the green leaves of spring.

Chestnut and oak woods on Rinkatasset, Concord, Massachusetts

U<small>P ASSABET.</small>

There are many crisped but colored leaves resting on the smooth surface of the Assabet, which for the most part is not stirred by a breath; but in some places, where the middle is rippled by a slight breeze, no leaves are seen, while the broad and perfectly smooth portions next the shore will be covered with them, as if by a current they were prevented from falling on the other parts. These leaves are chiefly of the red maple, with some white maple, etc. To be sure, they hardly begin to conceal the river, unless in some quiet coves, yet they remind me of ditches in swamps, whose surfaces are often quite concealed by leaves now. The waves made by my boat cause them to rustle, and both by sounds and sights I am reminded that I am in the very midst of the fall.

Methinks the reflections are never purer and more distinct than now at the season of the fall of the leaf, just before the cool twilight has come, when the air has a finer grain. Just as our mental reflections are more distinct at this season of the year, when the evenings grow cool and lengthen and our winter evenings with their brighter fires may be said to begin. And painted ducks, too, often come and sail or float amid the painted leaves.

A<small>VERY STILL</small>, warm, bright, clear afternoon. Our boat so small and low that we are close to the water.

The muskrats all the way are now building their houses, about two thirds done. They are of an oval form (looking down on them), sloping upward from the smaller end, by which the rat apparently ascends, and composed of mouthfuls of pontederia leaf-stems (now dead), the capillaceous roots or leaves of the water-marigold(?) and other capillaceous-leaved water-plants, flag-root, a plant which looks like a cock's tail or a peacock's feather in form, clamshells, etc., sometimes rising from amidst the dead pontederia stems or resting on the button-bushes or the willows. The mouthfuls are disposed in layers successively smaller, form-

Reflection in Assabet River, Concord, Massachusetts

Muskrat cabin, west side of Carlisle Beach, Concord, Massachusetts

ing a somewhat conical mound. Seen at this stage they show some art and a good deal of labor. We pulled one to pieces to examine the inside. There was a small cavity, which might hold two or three full-grown muskrats, just above the level of the water, quite wet and of course dark and narrow, communicating immediately with a gallery under water. There were a few pieces of the white root of some waterplant—perhaps a pontederia or a lily root—in it. There they dwell, in close contiguity to the water itself, always in a wet apartment, in a wet coat never changed, with immeasurable water in the cellar, through which is the only exit. They have reduced life to a lower scale than Diogenes. Certainly they do not fear cold, ague, or con-

sumption. Think of bringing up a family in such a place,—worse than a Broad Street cellar. But probably these are not their breeding-places. The muskrat and the fresh-water mussel are very native to our river. The Indian, their human compeer, has departed. There is a settler whom our low-lands and our fogs do not hurt. One of the fishermen speared one last night. How long has the muskrat dined on mussels? The river mud itself will have the ague as soon as he. What occasion has he for a dentist? Their unfinished, rapidly rising nests look now like truncated cones. They seem to be all building at once in different parts of the river, and to have advanced equally far.

Barrett's Mill Pond, Concord, Massachusetts

WALKED along the dam and the broad bank of the canal with Hosmer. He thought this bank proved that there were strong men here a hundred years ago or more, and that probably they used wooden shovels edged with iron, and perchance home-made, to make that bank with, for he remembered and had used them. Thus rapidly we skip back to the implements of the savage. Some call them "shod shovels."

RIDE to Sam Barrett's mill.
    Am pleased again to see the cobweb drapery of the mill.

Each fine line hanging in festoons from the timbers overhead and on the sides, and on the discarded machinery lying about, is covered and greatly enlarged by a coating of meal, by which its curve is revealed, like the twigs under their ridges of snow in winter. It is like the tassels and tapestry of counterpane and dimity in a lady's bedchamber, and I pray that the cobwebs may not have been brushed away from the mills which I visit. It is as if I were aboard a man-of-war, and this were the fine "rigging" of the mill, the sails being taken in. All things in the mill wear the same livery or drapery, down to the miller's hat and coat. I knew Barrett forty rods off in the cranberry meadow by the meal on his hat.

Cobwebs in Barrett's Mill, Concord, Massachusetts

How pleasant to walk over beds of these fresh, crisp, and rustling fallen leaves,—young hyson, green tea, clean, crisp, and wholesome! How beautiful they go to their graves! how gently lay themselves down and turn to mould!—painted of a thousand hues and fit to make the beds of us living. So they troop to their graves, light and frisky. They put on no weeds. Merrily they go scampering over the earth, selecting their graves, whispering all through the woods about it. They that waved so loftily, how contentedly they return to dust again and are laid low, resigned to lie and decay at the foot of the tree and afford nourishment to new generations of their kind, as well as to flutter on high! How they are mixed up, all species,—oak and maple and chestnut and birch! They are about to add a leaf's breadth to the depth of the soil. We are all the richer for their decay. Nature is not cluttered with them. She is a perfect husbandman; she stores them all.

I cannot easily dismiss the subject of the fallen leaves. How densely they cover and conceal the water for several feet in width, under and amid the alders and button-bushes and maples along the shore of the river,—still light, tight, and dry boats, dense cities of boats, their fibres not relaxed by the waters, undulating and rustling, though fading, tints,—of hues that might make the fame of teas,—dried on great Nature's coppers. And then see this great fleet of scattered leaf boats, still tight and dry, each one curled up on every side by the sun's skill, like boats of hide, scarcely moving in the sluggish current,—like the great fleets with which you mingle on entering some great mart, some New York which we are all approaching together. Or else they are slowly moving round in some great eddy which the river makes, where the water is deep and the current is wearing into the bank. How gently each has been deposited on the water! No violence has been used toward them yet. But next the shore, as thick as foam they float, and when you turn your prow that way, list! what a rustling of the crisped waves! Wet grounds about the edges of swamps look dry with them, and many a wet foot you get in consequence.

Consider what a vast crop is thus annually shed upon the earth. This, more than any mere grain or seed, is the great harvest of the year. This annual decay and death, this dying by inches, before the whole tree at last lies down and turns to soil. As trees shed their leaves, so deer their horns, and men their hair or nails. The year's great crop. I am more interested in it than in the English grass alone or in the corn. It prepares the virgin mould for future cornfields on which the earth fattens. They teach us how to die. How many flutterings before they rest quietly in their graves! A myriad wrappers for germinating seeds. By what subtle chemistry they will mount up again, climbing by the sap in the trees. The ground is all parti-colored with them.

THE WHITE BIRCHES being now generally bare, they stand along the east side of Heywood's meadow slender, parallel white stems, revealed in a pretty reddish maze produced by their fine branches. It is a lesser and denser smoke(?) than the maple one. The branches must be thick, like those of maples and birches, to give the effect of smoke, and most trees have fewer and coarser branches, or do not grow in such dense masses.

THE THISTLES which I now see have their heads recurved, which at least saves their down from so great a soaking. But when I pull out the down, the seed is for the most part left in the receptacle (?), in regular order there, like the pricks in a thimble. A slightly convex surface. The seeds set like cartridges in a circular cartridge-box, in hollow cylinders which look like circles *crowded* into more or less of a diamond, pentagonal, or hexagonal form. The perfectly dry and bristly involucre which hedges them round, so repulsive externally, is very neat and attractive within,—as smooth and tender toward its charge as it is rough and prickly externally toward the foes that might do it injury. It is a hedge of imbricated thin and narrow leafets of a light-brown color, beautifully glossy like silk, a most fit receptacle for the delicate downy parachutes of the seed, a cradle lined with silk or satin. The latter are kept dry under this unsuspected silky or satiny ceiling, whose old and weather-worn and rough outside alone we see, like a mossy roof, little suspecting the delicate and glossy lining. I know of no object more unsightly to a careless glance than an empty thistle-head, yet, if you examine it closely, it may remind you of the silk-lined cradle in which a prince was rocked. Thus that which seemed a mere brown and worn-out relic of the summer, sinking into the earth by the roadside, turns out to be a precious casket.

A "mist" of birches in river pasture below Chelmsford Bridge, Billerica, Massachusetts

Thistle ball, Hiram, Maine

THE *Asclepias Cornuti* pods are now apparently in the midst of discounting. They point at various angles with the stem like a flourish. The pretty brown  fishes have loosened and lifted their scales somewhat, are bristling a little. Or, further advanced, the outer part of the  down of the upper seeds is blown loose, while they are still retained by the ends of the middle portion in loops attached to the core. These white tufts, ready to burst and take to flight on the least jar, show afar as big as your fist. There they dangle and flutter, till they are quite dry and the wind rises. Others again are open and empty, except of the brown core, and you see what a delicate smooth white (slightly cream-colored) lining this casket has.

Milkweed pods, Tyngsboro, Massachusetts

Hubbard's great oak, Concord, Massachusetts

How handsome the great red oak acorns now! I stand under the tree on Emerson's lot. They are still falling. I heard one fall into the water as I approached, and thought that a musquash had plunged. They strew the ground and the bottom of the river thickly, and while I stand here I hear one strike the boughs with force as it comes down, and drop into the water. The part that was covered by the cup is whitish-woolly. How munificent is Nature to create this profusion of wild fruit, as it were merely to gratify our eyes! Though inedible they are more wholesome to my immortal part, and stand by me longer, than the fruits which I eat. If they had been plums or chestnuts I should have eaten them on the spot and probably forgotten them.

They would have afforded only a momentary gratification, but being acorns, I remember, and as it were *feed* on, them still. They are untasted fruits forever in store for me. I know not of their flavor as yet. That is postponed to some still unimagined winter evening. These which we admire but do not eat are nuts of the gods. When time is no more we shall crack them. I cannot help liking them better than horse-chestnuts, which are of a similar color, not only because they are of a much handsomer form, but because they are indigenous. What hale, plump fellows they are! They can afford not to be useful to me, nor to know me or be known by me. They go their way, I go mine, and it turns out that sometimes I go *after* them.

WE WERE NOW fairly on the Cape, which extends from Sandwich eastward thirty-five miles, and thence north and northwest thirty more, in all sixty-five, and has an average breadth of about five miles. . . .

Hitchcock conjectures that the ocean has, in course of time, eaten out Boston Harbor and other bays in the mainland, and that the minute fragments have been deposited by the currents at a distance from the shore, and formed this sand-bank. Above the sand, if the surface is subjected to agricultural tests, there is found to be a thin layer of soil gradually diminishing from Barnstable to Truro, where it ceases; but there are many holes and rents in this weather-beaten garment not likely to be stitched in time, which reveal the naked flesh of the Cape, and its extremity is completely bare.

South, over Sound from South Chatham, Cape Cod, Massachusetts

The NEXT MORNING, Thursday, October 11, it rained as hard as ever; but we were determined to proceed on foot, nevertheless. We first made some inquiries, with regard to the practicability of walking up the shore on the Atlantic side to Provincetown, whether we should meet with any creeks or marshes to trouble us. Higgins said that there was no obstruction, and that it was not much farther than by the road, but he thought that we should find it very "heavy" walking in the sand; it was bad enough in the road, a horse would sink in up to the fetlocks there. But there was one man at the tavern who had walked it, and he said that we could go very well, though it was sometimes inconvenient and even dangerous walking under the bank, when there was a great tide, with an easterly wind, which caused the sand to cave.

Along the beach at Wellfleet Bluffs, Cape Cod, Massachusetts

THE MOST FOREIGN and picturesque structures on the Cape, to an inlander, not excepting the salt-works, are the windmills,—gray-looking, octagonal towers, with long timbers slanting to the ground in the rear, and there resting on a cart-wheel, by which their fans are turned round to face the wind. These appeared also to serve in some measure for props against its force. A great circular rut was worn around the building by the wheel. The neighbors who assemble to turn the mill to the wind are likely to know which way it blows, without a weather-cock. They looked loose and slightly locomotive, like huge wounded birds, trailing a wing or a leg, and reminded one of pictures of the Netherlands. Being on elevated ground, and high in themselves, they serve as landmarks,—for there are no tall trees, or other objects commonly, which can be seen at a distance in the horizon; though the outline of the land itself is so firm and distinct, that an insignificant cone, or even precipice of sand, is visible at a great distance from over the sea. Sailors making the land commonly steer either by the windmills, or the meeting-houses. In the country, we are obliged to steer by the meeting-houses alone. Yet the meeting-house is a kind of windmill, which runs one day in seven, turned either by the winds of doctrine or public opinion, or more rarely by the winds of Heaven, where another sort of grist is ground, of which, if it be not all bran or musty, if it be not *plaster*, we trust to make bread of life.

Distant view of old windmill, Chatham, Cape Cod, Massachusetts

Old windmill (1797), Chatham, Cape Cod, Massachusetts

THE TREES were, if possible, rarer than the houses, excepting apple trees, of which there were a few small orchards in the hollows. These were either narrow and high, with flat tops, having lost their side branches, like huge plum bushes growing in exposed situations, or else dwarfed and branching immediately at the ground, like quince bushes. They suggested that, under like circumstances, all trees would at last acquire like habits of growth. I afterward saw on the Cape many full-grown apple trees not higher than a man's head; one whole orchard, indeed, where all the fruit could have been gathered by a man standing on the ground; but you could hardly creep beneath the trees.

Some, which the owners told me were twenty years old, were only three and a half feet high, spreading at six inches from the ground five feet each way, and, being withal surrounded with boxes of tar to catch the canker-worms, they looked like plants in flower-pots, and as if they might be taken into the house in the winter. In another place, I saw some not much larger than currant bushes; yet the owner told me that they had borne a barrel and a half of apples

that fall. If they had been placed close together, I could have cleared them all at a jump. I measured some near the Highland Light in Truro, which had been taken from the shrubby woods thereabouts when young, and grafted. One, which had been set ten years, was on an average eighteen inches high, and spread nine feet, with a flat top. It had borne one bushel of apples two years before. Another, probably twenty years old from the seed, was five feet high, and spread eighteen feet, branching, as usual, at the ground, so that you could not creep under it. This bore a barrel of apples two years before.

The owner of these trees invariably used the personal pronoun in speaking of them; as, "I got *him* out of the woods, but *he* does n't bear." The largest that I saw in that neighborhood was nine feet high to the topmost leaf, and spread thirty-three feet, branching at the ground five ways.

In one yard I observed a single, very healthy-looking tree, while all the rest were dead or dying. The occupant said that his father had manured all but that one with blackfish.

Apple tree, North Truro, Cape Cod, Massachusetts

HAVING WALKED about eight miles since we struck the beach, and passed the boundary between Wellfleet and Truro, a stone post in the sand,—for even this sand comes under the jurisdiction of one town or another,—we turned inland over barren hills and valleys, whither the sea, for some reason, did not follow us, and, tracing up a Hollow, discovered two or three sober-looking houses within half a mile, uncommonly near the eastern coast. Their garrets were apparently so full of chambers, that their roofs could hardly lie down straight, and we did not doubt that there was room for us there. Houses near the sea are generally low and broad. These were a story and a half high; but if you merely counted the windows in their gable ends, you would think that there were many stories more, or, at any rate, that the half-story was the only one thought worthy of being illustrated.

Old houses on Atwood Street, Chatham, Cape Cod, Massachusetts

BEFORE the land rose out of the ocean, and became *dry* land, chaos reigned; and between high and low water mark, where she is partially disrobed and rising, a sort of chaos reigns still, which only anomalous creatures can inhabit. Mackerel gulls were all the while flying over our heads and amid the breakers, sometimes two white ones pursuing a black one; quite at home in the storm, though they are as delicate organizations as sea-jellies and mosses; and we saw that they were adapted to their circumstances rather by their spirits than their bodies. Theirs must be an essentially wilder, that is, less human, nature, than that of larks and robins. Their note was like the sound of some vibrating metal, and harmonized well with the scenery and the roar of the surf, as if one had rudely touched the strings of the lyre, which ever lies on the shore; a ragged shred of ocean music tossed aloft on the spray.

Sunrise from Cahoon's Hollow, Cape Cod, Massachusetts

Cloud effect over Pleasant Bay, South Orleans, Cape Cod, Massachusetts

THE ALMOST UNIVERSAL bareness and smoothness of the landscape were as agreeable as novel, making it so much the more like the deck of a vessel. We saw vessels sailing south into the Bay, on the one hand, and north along the Atlantic shore, on the other, all with an aft wind.

THE OCEAN is but a larger lake. At midsummer you may sometimes see a strip of glassy smoothness on it, a few rods in width and many miles long, as if the surface there were covered with a thin pellicle of oil, just as on a country pond; a sort of standstill, you would say, at the meeting or parting of two currents of air (if it does not rather mark the unrippled steadiness of a current of water beneath), for sailors tell of the ocean and land breeze meeting between the fore and aft sails of a vessel, while the latter are full, the former being suddenly taken aback. Daniel Webster, in one of his letters describing blue-fishing off Martha's Vineyard, referring to those smooth places, which fishermen and sailors call "slicks," says:

"We met with them yesterday, and our boatman made for them, whenever discovered. He said they were caused by the blue-fish chopping up their prey. That is to say, those voracious fellows get into a school of menhaden, which are too large to swallow whole, and they bite them into pieces to suit their tastes. And the oil from this butchery, rising to the surface, makes the 'slick.'"

Yet this same placid ocean, as civil now as a city's harbor, a place for ships and commerce, will ere long be lashed into sudden fury, and all its caves and cliffs will resound with tumult. It will ruthlessly heave these vessels to and fro, break them in pieces in its sandy or stony jaws, and deliver their crews to sea-monsters. It will play with them like seaweed, distend them like dead frogs, and carry them about, now high, now low, to show to the fishes, giving them a nibble. This gentle ocean will toss and tear the rag of a man's body like the father of mad bulls, and his relatives may be seen seeking the remnants for weeks along the strand. From some quiet inland hamlet they have rushed weeping to the unheard-of shore, and now stand uncertain where a sailor has recently been buried amid the sand-hills.

Sunrise from harbor, Chatham, Cape Cod, Massachusetts.

To the fisherman, the Cape itself is a sort of store-ship laden with supplies,—a safer and larger craft which carries the women and children, the old men and the sick, and indeed sea phrases are as common on it as on board a vessel. Thus is it ever with a seagoing people. The old Northmen used to speak of the "keel-ridge" of the country, that is, the ridge of the Doffrafield Mountains, as if the land were a boat turned bottom up. I was frequently reminded of the Northmen here. The inhabitants of the Cape are often at once farmers and sea-rovers; they are more than vikings or kings of the bays, for their sway extends over the open sea also.

Fish trap and boat, Harwich Port, Cape Cod, Massachusetts

Early the next morning I walked into a fish-house near our hotel, where three or four men were engaged in trundling out the pickled fish on barrows, and spreading them to dry. They told me that a vessel had lately come in from the Banks with forty-four thousand cod-fish. Timothy Dwight says that, just before he arrived at Provincetown, "a schooner came in from the Great Bank with fifty-six thousand fish, almost one thousand five hundred quintals, taken in a single voyage; the main deck being, on her return, eight inches under water in calm weather."

The cod in this fish-house, just out of the pickle, lay packed several feet deep, and three or four men stood on them in cowhide boots, pitching them on to the barrows with an instrument which had a single iron point. One young man, who chewed tobacco, spat on the fish repeatedly. Well, sir, thought I, when that older man sees you he will speak to you. But presently I saw the older man do the same thing. It reminded me of the figs of Smyrna.

"How long does it take to cure these fish?" I asked.

"Two good drying days, sir," was the answer.

I walked across the street again into the hotel to breakfast, and mine host inquired if I would take "hashed fish or beans." I took beans, though they never were a favorite dish of mine.

Old fish house, Pleasant Bay, South Orleans, Cape Cod, Massachusetts

To BATEMAN'S POND.

Row up Assabet as far as the Pokelogan, thence on foot. It is very pleasant and cheerful nowadays, when the brown and withered leaves strew the ground and almost every plant is fallen or withered, to come upon a patch of polypody on some rocky hillside in the woods,—as in abundance on hillside between Calla Swamp and Bateman's Pond, and still more same hillside east of the callas,—where, in the midst of the dry and rustling leaves, defying frost, it stands so freshly green and full of life. The mere greenness, which was not remarkable in the summer, is positively interesting now. My thoughts are with the polypody a long time after my body has passed. The brakes, the sarsaparilla, the osmundas, the Solomon's-seals, the lady's-slippers have long since withered and fallen. The huckleberries and blueberries, too, have lost their leaves. The forest floor is covered with a thick coat of moist brown leaves. But what is that perennial and springlike verdure that clothes the rocks, of small green plumes pointing various ways? It is the cheerful community of the polypody. It survives at least as the type of vegetation, to remind us of the spring which shall not fail. These are the green pastures where I browse now. Why is not this form copied by our sculptors instead of the foreign acanthus leaves and bays? The sight of this unwithering green leaf excites me like red at some seasons. Are not the wood frogs the philosophers who walk (?) in these groves? Methinks I imbibe a cool, composed, frog-like philosophy when I behold them. I don't care for acanthus leaves; they are far-fetched. I do love this form, however, and would like to see it painted or sculptured, whether on your marble or my butter. How fit for a tuft about the base of a column!

Polypody fern, Bateman's Pond, Concord, Massachusetts

Old stump, Concord, Massachusetts

To PINE HILL *via* Spanish Brook.

I leave the railroad at Walden Crossing and follow the
path to Spanish Brook. How swift Nature is to repair the
damage that man does! When he has cut down a tree and
left only a white-topped and bleeding stump, she comes at
once to the rescue with her chemistry, and covers it decently
with a fresh coat of gray, and in course of time she adds
a thick coat of green cup and bright cockscomb lichens,
and it becomes an object of new interest to the lover of
nature! Suppose it were always to remain a raw stump
instead! It becomes a shell on which this humble vegetation
spreads and displays itself, and we forget the death of the
larger in the life of the less.

SAW MILL BROOK is peculiar among our brooks as a mountain brook. For a short distance it reminds me of runs I have seen in New Hampshire. A brawling little stream tumbling through a rocky wood, ever down and down. Where the wood has been cleared, it is almost covered with the rubbish which the woodchoppers have left, the fine tree-tops, which no one cared to make into fagots. It was quite a discovery when I first came upon this brawling mountain stream in Concord woods. Rising out of an obscure meadow in the woods, for some fifty or sixty rods of its course it is a brawling mountain stream in our quiet Concord woods, as much obstructed by rocks—rocks out of all proportion to its tiny stream—as a brook can well be. And the rocks are bared throughout the wood on either side, as if a torrent had anciently swept through here; so unlike the after character of the stream. Who would have thought that, on tracing it up from where it empties into the larger Mill Brook in the open peat meadows, it would conduct him to such a headlong and impetuous youth. Perchance it should be called a "force." It suggests what various moods may attach to the same character. Ah, if I but knew that some minds which flow so muddily in the lowland portion of their course, when they cross the highways, tumbled thus impetuously and musically, mixed themselves with the air in foam, but a little way back in the woods! that these dark and muddy pools, where only the pout and the leech are to be found, issued from pure trout streams higher up! that the man's thoughts ever flowed as sparkling mountain water, that trout there loved to glance through his dimples, where the witch-hazel hangs over his stream!

Saw Mill Brook, Concord, Massachusetts

Willow row, over Mill Brook from Lowell Road, Concord, Massachusetts

THE STILLNESS of the woods and fields is remarkable at this season of the year. There is not even the creak of a cricket to be heard. Of myriads of dry shrub oak leaves, not one rustles. Your own breath can rustle them, yet the breath of heaven does not suffice to. The trees have the aspect of waiting for winter. The autumnal leaves have lost their color; they are now truly sere, dead, and the woods wear a sombre color. Summer and harvest are over. The hickories, birches, chestnuts, no less than the maples, have lost their leaves. The sprouts, which had shot up so vigorously to repair the damage which the choppers had done, have stopped short for the winter. Everything stands silent and expectant. If I listen, I hear only the note of a chickadee,—our most common and I may say native bird, most identified with our forests,—or perchance the scream of a jay, or perchance from the solemn depths of these woods I hear tolling far away the knell of one departed. Thought rushes in to fill the vacuum. As you walk, however, the partridge still bursts away. The silent, dry, almost leafless, certainly fruitless woods. You wonder what cheer that bird can find in them. The partridge bursts away from the foot of a shrub oak like its own dry fruit, immortal bird! This sound still startles us. Dry goldenrods, now turned gray and white, lint our clothes as we walk. And the drooping, downy seed-vessels of the epilobium remind us of the summer. Perchance you will meet with a few solitary asters in the dry fields, with a little color left. The sumach is stripped of everything but its cone of red berries.

This is a peculiar season, peculiar for its stillness. The crickets have ceased their song. The few birds are well-nigh silent. The tinted and gay leaves are now sere and dead, and the woods wear a sombre aspect. A carpet of snow under the pines and shrub oaks will make it look more cheerful. Very few plants have now their spring. But thoughts still spring in man's brain. There are no flowers nor berries to speak of. The grass begins to die at top. In the morning it is stiff with frost. Ice has been discovered in somebody's tub very early this morn, of the thickness of a dollar. The flies are betwixt life and death. The wasps come into the houses and settle on the walls and windows. All insects go into crevices. The fly is entangled in a web and struggles vainly to escape, but there is no spider to secure him; the corner of the pane is a deserted camp. When I lived in the woods the wasps came by thousands to my lodge in November, as to winter quarters, and settled on my windows and on the walls over my head, sometimes deterring visitors from entering. Each morning, when they were numbed with cold, I swept some of them out. But I did not trouble myself to get rid of them. They never molested me, though they bedded with me, and they gradually disappeared into what crevices I do not know, avoiding winter. I saw a squash-bug go slowly behind a clapboard to avoid winter. As some of these melon seeds come up in the garden again in the spring, so some of these squash-bugs come forth. The flies are for a long time in a somnambulic state. They have too little energy or *vis vitæ* to clean their wings or heads, which are covered with dust. They buzz and bump their heads against the windows two or three times a day, or lie on their backs in a trance, and that is all,— two or three short spurts. One of these mornings we shall hear that Mr. Minott had to break the ice to water his cow. And so it will go on till the ground freezes. If the race had never lived through a winter, what would they think was coming?

Road through woods, Concord, Massachusetts

Old time quarry in Easterbrooks Country, Concord, Massachusetts

THE STONE at those quarries strikes northeasterly and southwesterly, or apparently with the rocks of Curly-pate, a third of a mile off. The strata appear to be nearly vertical. In the most southwesterly quarry, I noticed in the side of an upright sliver of rock, where the limestone had formerly been blasted off, the bottom of the nearly perpendicular hole which had been drilled for that purpose, two or three inches deep and about two and a half feet from the ground.

In this I found two fresh chestnuts, a dozen or more amphicarpæa seeds, as many apparently either prinos (?) or rose (?) seeds (single seeds and fresh), and several fresh barberry seeds mixed with a little earth and rubbish. What placed them there? Squirrel, mouse, jay, or crow? At first I thought that a quadruped could hardly have reached this hole, but probably it could easily, and it was a very cunning place for such a deposit.

I LOOK SOUTH from the Cliff. The westering sun just out of sight behind the hill. Its rays from those bare twigs across the pond are bread and cheese to me. So many oak leaves have fallen that the white birch stems are more distinct amid the young oaks; I see to the bone. See those brave birches prepared to stand the winter through on the hillsides. They never sing, "What's this dull town to me?" The maples skirting the meadows (in dense phalanxes) look like light infantry advanced for a swamp fight. Ah, dear *November*, ye must be sacred to the *Nine* surely.

Leaning birches on north shore of Flint's Pond, Lincoln, Massachusetts

I SEE in E. Hubbard's gray oak wood, four rods from the old wall line and two or three rods over the brow of the hill, an apparent downy woodpecker's nest in a dead white oak stub some six feet high. It is made as far as I can see, like that which I have, but looks quite fresh, and I see, by the very numerous fresh white chips of dead wood scattered *over* the recently fallen leaves beneath, that it must have been made since the leaves fell. Could it be a nuthatch or chickadee's work?

Old stump and woodpecker's hole, Corner Spring Woods, Concord, Massachusetts

Nine Acre Corner, Concord, Massachusetts

Maynard's yard and frontage, and all his barns and fences, are singularly neat and substantial, and the highroad is in effect converted into a private way through his grounds. It suggests unspeakable peace and happiness. Yet, strange to tell, I noticed that he had a tiger instead of a cock for a vane on his barn, and he himself looked overworked. He had allowed the surviving forest trees to grow into ancestral trees about his premises, and so attach themselves to him as if he had planted them. The dusty highway was so subdued that it seemed as if it were lost there. He had all but stretched a bar across it. Each traveller must have felt some misgivings, as if he were trespassing.

However, the farmer's life expresses only such content as an ox in his yard chewing the cud.

What though your hands are numb with cold, your sense of enjoyment is not benumbed. You cannot now find an apple but it is sweet to taste.

Simply to see to a distant horizon through a clear air,— the fine outline of a distant hill or a blue mountain-top through some new vista,—this is wealth enough for one afternoon.

First Andromeda Pond looking south, Concord, Massachusetts

Tʜᴇsᴇ ᴀɴᴅʀᴏᴍᴇᴅᴀ sᴡᴀᴍᴘs charmed me more than twenty years ago,—I knew not why,—and I called them "a moccasin-print."

The *Fringilla hyemalis* appear to be flitting about in a more lively manner on account of the cold. They go off with a twitter from the low weeds and bushes. Nowadays birds are so rare I am wont to mistake them at first for a leaf or mote [?] blown off from the trees or bushes.

"A Precipice of Pine" on J. P. Brown's land, Concord, Massachusetts

A RATHER COLD and windy afternoon, with some snow not yet melted on the ground. Under the south side of the hill between Brown's and Tarbell's, in a warm nook, disturbed three large gray squirrels and some partridges, who had all sought out this bare and warm place. While the squirrels hid themselves in the tree-tops, I sat on an oak stump by an old cellar-hole and mused. This squirrel is always an unexpectedly large animal to see frisking about. My eye wanders across the valley to the pine woods which fringe the opposite side, and in their aspect my eye finds something which addresses itself to my nature. Methinks that in my mood I was asking Nature to give me a sign. I do not know exactly what it was that attracted my eye. I experienced a transient gladness, at any rate, at something which I saw. I am sure that my eye rested with pleasure on the white pines, now reflecting a silvery light, the infinite stories of their boughs, tier above tier, a sort of basaltic structure, a crumbling precipice of pine horizontally stratified. Each pine is like a great green feather stuck in the ground. A myriad white pine boughs extend themselves horizontally, one above and behind another, each bearing its burden of silvery sunlight, with darker seams between them, as if it were a great crumbling piny precipice thus stratified. On this my eyes pastured, while the squirrels were up the trees behind me. That, at any rate, it was that I got by my afternoon walk, a certain recognition from the pine, some congratulation. Where is my home? It is indistinct as an old cellar-hole, now a faint indentation merely in a farmer's field, which he has plowed into and rounded off its edges years ago, and I sit by the old site on the stump of an oak which once grew there. Such is the nature where we have lived.

TEXTUAL SOURCES

The text is taken from the following volumes of *The Writings of Henry David Thoreau* (Boston and New York: Houghton Mifflin, 1906): *Journal*, Bradford Torrey, ed.; *The Maine Woods; Cape Cod and Miscellanies*. Unless otherwise indicated, all references are to volumes of the *Journal*.

LOCATIONS AND DATES OF PHOTOGRAPHS

Thoreau Country

was designed by Klaus Gemming, New Haven, Connecticut,
and printed in fine-screen duotone process with varnish
by George Rice and Sons, Los Angeles, California,
on 100-lb. Consolidated Centura Dull coated paper.
The text was set in Linotype Janson and the display lines
in Centaur and Arrighi by Finn Typographic Service,
Stamford, Connecticut. The book was bound by Banta West,
Sparks, Nevada, and its production was supervised by
David Charlsen, San Francisco, California. The map of
Thoreau Country is by Sam Bryant, Marblehead, Massachusetts.

Sierra Club Books